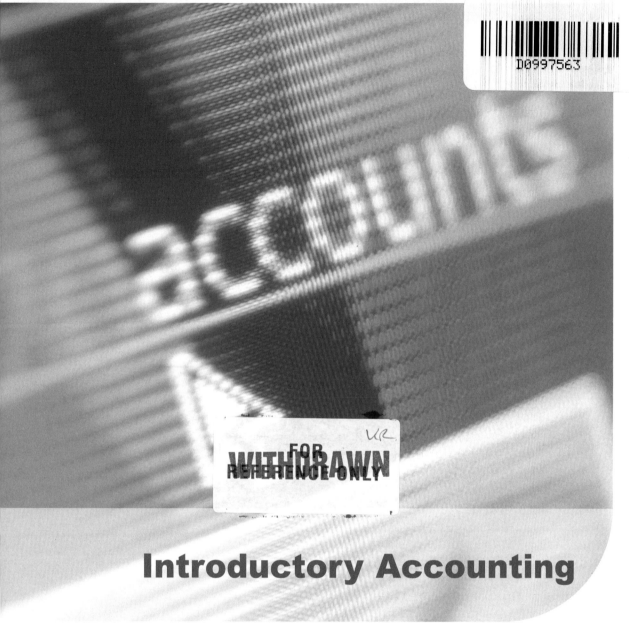

Introductory Accounting

Workbook

AAT Diploma Pathway Unit 30

David Cox

Michael Fa

osborne
BOOKS

Published by Osborne Books Limited
Unit 1B Everoak Estate
Bromyard Road
Worcester WR2 5HP
Tel 01905 748071
Email books@osbornebooks.co.uk
Website www.osbornebooks.co.uk

Design by Richard Holt
Cover image from Getty Images

Printed by CPI Antony Rowe Limited, Chippenham

British Library Cataloguing in Publication Data
A catalogue record for this book is available from the British Library

ISBN 978 1905777 013

Contents

workbook activities

practice examinations

appendix

Acknowledgements

The authors wish to thank the following for their help with the editing and production of the book: Mike Gilbert, Rosemarie Griffiths, Claire McCarthy and Jon Moore. Special thanks go to Roger Petheram, Series Editor, for reading, checking and advising on the development of this text. The publisher is indebted to the Association of Accounting Technicians for its generous help and advice to our authors and editors during the preparation of this text, and for permission to reproduce assessment material which has formed the basis for two of the practice Examinations.

Authors

David Cox has more than twenty years' experience teaching accountancy students over a wide range of levels. Formerly with the Management and Professional Studies Department at Worcester College of Technology, he now lectures on a freelance basis and carries out educational consultancy work in accountancy studies. He is author and joint author of a number of textbooks in the areas of accounting, finance and banking.

Michael Fardon has extensive teaching experience of a wide range of banking, business and accountancy courses at Worcester College of Technology. He now specialises in writing business and financial texts and is General Editor at Osborne Books. He is also an educational consultant and has worked extensively in the areas of vocational business curriculum development.

Introduction

Introductory Accounting Workbook is designed to be used alongside Osborne Books'
Introductory Accounting Tutorial and is ideal for student use in the classroom, at home
and on distance learning courses. Both the *Tutorial* and the *Workbook* are designed for
students preparing for assessment for the AAT Diploma Pathway Unit 30
'Introductory Accounting'.

Introductory Accounting Workbook is divided into two sections: Workbook Activities
and Practice Examinations.

Workbook Activities

Workbook activities are self-contained exercises which are designed to be used to
supplement the activities in the tutorial text. A number of them are more extended than
the exercises in the tutorial and provide useful practice for students preparing for the
Examination.

Practice Examinations

The Unit 30 Examination is in a very specific style. The more that students practise
answering these types of task, the more competent and confident they will become.
There are three practice papers in this book, all of which exactly match the format of
the Unit assessment. Some of the tasks are taken from original AAT questions and
some have been written by the authors of this text. Osborne Books is grateful to the
AAT for their kind permission to reproduce tasks from published past papers.

answers

The answers to the tasks and exams in the *Workbook* are available in a separate *Tutor
Pack*. Contact the Osborne Books Sales Office on 01905 748071 for details or obtain
an order form from www.osbornebooks.co.uk.

www.osbornebooks.co.uk

Visit the Osborne Books website, which contains Resources sections for tutors and
students. These sections provide a wealth of free material, including downloadable
documents and layouts and assistance with other areas of study.

Workbook activities

■ This section contains activities which are suitable for use with the individual chapters of *Introductory Accounting Tutorial* from Osborne Books.

■ Activities have not been included for Chapters 8 and 15. This is because they are supplementary 'background' chapters on the subjects of Communication and Law and are adequately covered in the Tutorial text and elsewhere in this workbook.

■ A number of the activities in this workbook require the completion of accounting records such as ledger accounts, daybooks and petty cash book. These three layouts may be photocopied from the Appendix (page 195). These and further examples of documents and layouts are also available as free downloads from www.osbornebooks.co.uk

1 INTRODUCTION TO ACCOUNTING

1.1 What is the difference between a sole trader, a partnership and a limited company in terms of the following factors?

- ownership of the business
- the ability to specialise in one area of the business
- liability for business debts
- the need to keep accounting records

Set out your answer in the form of a table with the above factors as headings.

1.2 Give three examples of revenue expenditure and three examples of capital expenditure.

1.3 The accounting records of Tom's sole trader business show the following account totals at the end of the year:

Capital (money invested by the owner)	£185,000
Business premises	£100,000
Bank overdraft (owed to the bank)	£80,000
Computers used in the business	£50,000
Stock held by the business	£75,000
Creditors (amounts owed by the business)	£20,000
Debtors (money owed to the business)	£60,000

(a) Sort the above accounts under the three categories set out below, and total each category:
- assets
- liabilities
- capital

(b) Insert the three totals into the accounting equation

assets   minus   liabilities   equals   capital

If the equation does not balance, check your categories in (a) above.

(c) Tom has increased the bank overdraft to buy more stock costing £10,000. Adjust the totals in the equation. It should still balance; if it does not, check your workings.

2 DOCUMENTS FOR GOODS AND SERVICES SUPPLIED

INTRODUCTION

You work as an accounts assistant at Compusupply Limited, a business which sells computer supplies such as disks and listing paper to a wide range of customers.

It is your job to process incoming orders which arrive in the form of purchase orders, faxes and telephoned orders.

You also deal with the accounting side of returned goods and you issue credit notes when credit is due.

You are also in charge of sending out statements.

You are authorised to issue invoices without reference to the accounts supervisor as long as the account is kept within its credit limit. You are required to refer any difficulties and likely excesses over credit limits to your supervisor.

Compusupply Limited normally operates a computer accounting system, but unfortunately the system has crashed and you have been asked to process all the necessary documents by hand until the hard disk has been repaired. The crash is a serious one, so you may be without the computer for over a week.

You have been given the following information:

CUSTOMER DETAILS (EXTRACTS FROM COMPUSUPPLY FILES)				
customer	account number	discount %	credit limit £	balance £
Andrews, R C	234	10	1000	750.00
Harber Employment Agency	341	10	1000	456.75
Case, Justin	209	10	1000	218.50
P C Mack Limited	197	20	5000	3190.00
Singh, I	222	10	1000	00.00
Singh, R, Retail	265	20	3500	2185.00
Townsend Litho	409	20	5000	4756.75
Zebra Designs Ltd	376	10	1000	487.50

COMPUSUPPLY CATALOGUE (EXTRACT)

code	product	unit price	£ (excl VAT)
OMHD10	OM 3.5 inch diskettes DSHD	boxes of 10	5.50
Z100	Zip 100MB cartridges	each	12.99
LP80	Computer listing paper 80 column	2000 sheet box	14.99
LP132	Computer listing paper 132 column	2000 sheet box	19.99
SQ44	Syquest disk 44MB	each	36.99
SQ88	Syquest disk 88MB	each	42.99
SQ200	Syquest disk 200MB	each	49.99
DB40	Floppy storage box (40 disks)	each	4.99
DB80	Floppy storage box (80 disks)	each	5.99
AG1	VDU anti-glare screen (mesh)	each	11.99
AG2	VDU anti-glare screen (glass)	each	19.99

ACTIVITIES

2.1   You have to check a batch of invoices to make sure the correct customer trade discount of 10% has been applied.

The totals before deduction of discount are:

(a)   £67.50

(b)   £45.00

(c)   £107.95

(d)   £12,567.95

(e)   £12.75

(f)   £89.00

(g)   £400.00

(h)   £17,450.50

(i)   £1.75

(j)   £30.33

You are to work out the net totals before VAT. Remember to round up or down to the nearest penny.

2.2   You have to check the VAT calculation on a further batch of invoices. The totals before VAT are:

(a)   £40.00

(b)   £8.00

(c)   £75.00

(d)   £675.50

You are to work out the VAT *and* the final total in each case. Remember to round VAT amounts down to the nearest penny in each case.

2.3   Your colleague reminds you that a settlement discount of 2.5% is due on the four invoices in the previous task. You are to adjust the VAT to allow for a settlement discount of 2.5% and recalculate the totals, but remembering that the net total shown on the invoice will *not* be reduced - only the VAT amount.

2.4   In the morning post there are three purchase orders. You are to complete invoices for all three orders. The date is 20 October 2007 and the invoices should be numbered consecutively from 309530. Blank invoices are printed on the pages that follow the purchase orders.

JUSTIN CASE *insurance services* 2 Oakfield Business Centre Letchfield LT1 7TR Tel 01903 273423	**PURCHASE ORDER**

TO

Compusupply Limited Unit 17 Elgar Estate, Broadfield, BR7 4ER	purchase order no 58345 date 17 October 2007

product code	quantity	description
LP80	2 boxes	Computer listing paper, 80 columns

Authorised   signature......*J Case*..date..........*17.10.07*...........

R SINGH RETAIL

2 The Crescent
Broadfield
BR6 3TR
Tel 01908 456291

PURCHASE ORDER

TO

Compusupply Limited
Unit 17 Elgar Estate,
Broadfield, BR7 4ER

purchase order no   353453

date   17 October 2007

product code	quantity	description
OMHD10	10	OM 3.5 inch floppy disks

Authorised   signature.......*R Singh*..................................date.............*17.10.07*..........

P C Mack Ltd

57 New Road
Broadfield
BR3 6TF
Tel 01908 456291

PURCHASE ORDER

TO

Compusupply Limited
Unit 17 Elgar Estate,
Broadfield, BR7 4ER

purchase order no 14535

date   15 October 2007

product code	quantity	description
SQ44	2	Syquest 44MB disks

Authorised   signature.......*Steve Gates*..................date.*15.10.07*.........

INVOICE
COMPUSUPPLY LIMITED

Unit 17 Elgar Estate, Broadfield, BR7 4ER
Tel 01908 765756 Fax 01908 765777 Email rob@compusupply.u-net.com
VAT Reg GB 0745 4689 13

invoice to

invoice no

account

your reference

date/tax point

product code	description	quantity	price	unit	total	discount %	net
					goods total		

terms
Net monthly
Carriage paid
E & OE

VAT	
TOTAL	

INVOICE
COMPUSUPPLY LIMITED

Unit 17 Elgar Estate, Broadfield, BR7 4ER
Tel 01908 765756 Fax 01908 765777 Email rob@compusupply.u-net.com
VAT Reg GB 0745 4689 13

invoice to

invoice no

account

your reference

date/tax point

product code	description	quantity	price	unit	total	discount %	net
					goods total		

terms
Net monthly
Carriage paid
E & OE

VAT	
TOTAL	

INVOICE

COMPUSUPPLY LIMITED

Unit 17 Elgar Estate, Broadfield, BR7 4ER
Tel 01908 765756 Fax 01908 765777 Email rob@compusupply.u-net.com
VAT Reg GB 0745 4689 13

invoice to

invoice no

account

your reference

date/tax point

product code	description	quantity	price	unit	total	discount %	net
					goods total		

terms
Net monthly
Carriage paid
E & OE

VAT	
TOTAL	

2.5 Check the invoice extracts shown below with the Catalogue and customer discount list, making sure that the details and the calculations are correct. Where there are errors, correct them in red ink.

Note: VAT is always rounded down to the nearest penny. No settlement discounts are involved.

(a) Invoice to R C Andrews

code	description	quantity	price	total	discount %	net
AG1	VDU anti-glare screen (glass)	1	19.99	19.99	20	15.99

goods total	15.99
VAT @ 17.5%	2.79
TOTAL	18.78

(b)   Invoice to I Singh

code	description	quantity	price	total	discount %	net
DB40	Floppy storage box (40)	4	4.99	19.96	10	15.97

goods total	15.97
VAT @ 17.5%	2.79
TOTAL	13.18

(c)   Invoice to Harber Employment Agency

code	description	quantity	price	total	discount %	net
OMHD10	OM 3.5 inch disks DSHD	10 boxes	5.50	55.00	20	44.00

goods total	44.00
VAT @ 17.5%	7.70
TOTAL	51.70

2.6   When you return from lunch there are two telephone messages for you:

> # telephone message
>
> **to**   *order processing*
>
> **date**   *20.10.07*   **time**   *13.45*
>
> *Townsend Litho telephoned. They want to order ten 200MB Syquest disks as soon as possible. Can you get them off by carrier today? Thanks. Sue.*

Townsend Litho is a well-established customer with a good record of paying on time.

> # telephone message
>
> **to**   *order processing*
>
> **date**   *20.10.07*   **time**   *13.45*
>
> *Zebra Designs called. They want a box of computer listing paper. 80 columns.*
>
> *Thanks. Hanif.*

On your return from lunch a colleague mentions that he thought he saw a notice in the local paper about Zebra Designs going 'bust'. You look in the official announcement column of the paper and see that your colleague is correct – a creditors' meeting is called for next Monday. Zebra Designs is in deep financial trouble.

You are to

(a)   State what you would do in response to the two telephone messages.

(b)   Describe the likely course of action taken by Compusupply in response to the two situations.

2.7   It is now a week later – 27 October 2007 – and the computer system is still not working, so you have to complete all documents by hand.

During the course of the day you receive two returns notes (printed on the next page)

You are to

(a)   Write down on the R Singh Retail returns note what has gone wrong with the order.

(b)   Complete the credit notes as requested (the documents are printed on the page following the returns notes).

R SINGH RETAIL

2 The Crescent
Broadfield
BR6 3TR
Tel 01908 456291

RETURNS NOTE

TO

Compusupply Limited
Unit 17 Elgar Estate,
Broadfield, BR7 4ER

returns note no   353453

date   22 October 2007

product code	quantity	description
OMHD10	9 boxes	OM 3.5 inch floppy disks

REASON FOR RETURN: too many disks sent — only 10 disks ordered. Please credit.

signature....*R Singh*............date..........*22.10.07*..........

P C Mack Ltd

57 New Road
Broadfield
BR3 6TF
Tel 01908 456291

RETURNS NOTE

TO

Compusupply Limited
Unit 17 Elgar Estate,
Broadfield, BR7 4ER

purchase order no 14535

date   23 October 2007

product code	quantity	description
SQ44	1	Syquest 44MB data disk.

REASON FOR RETURN: faulty disk. Please credit.

signature.................*Steve Gates*...............date..........*23.10.07*..........

━━━ CREDIT NOTE ━━━
COMPUSUPPLY LIMITED
Unit 17 Elgar Estate, Broadfield, BR7 4ER
Tel 01908 765756 Fax 01908 765777 Email rob@compusupply.u-net.com
VAT Reg GB 0745 4689 13

to

credit note no

account

your reference

our invoice

date/tax point

product code	description	quantity	price	unit	total	discount %	net
					goods total		

REASON FOR CREDIT:

goods total	
VAT	
TOTAL	

━━━ CREDIT NOTE ━━━
COMPUSUPPLY LIMITED
Unit 17 Elgar Estate, Broadfield, BR7 4ER
Tel 01908 765756 Fax 01908 765777 Email rob@compusupply.u-net.com
VAT Reg GB 0745 4689 13

to

credit note no

account

your reference

our invoice

date/tax point

product code	description	quantity	price	unit	total	discount %	net
					goods total		

REASON FOR CREDIT:

goods total	
VAT	
TOTAL	

2.8 It is now 31 October. The computer accounts package has been fixed and will start operating again from Monday 3 November. In the meantime you have to make out the customer statements. Using the start-of-month balances and all the transactions during the month, complete statements for R Singh Retail, P C Mack Limited and Justin Case. The statements are printed in the text.

The two payments you have received for these customers is a cheque for £218.50 from Justin Case on October 7 and a cheque for £3190.00 from P C Mack Limited on October 10.

STATEMENT

COMPUSUPPLY LIMITED

Unit 17 Elgar Estate, Broadfield, BR7 4ER
Tel 01908 765756 Fax 01908 765777 Email rob@compusupply.u-net.com
VAT Reg GB 0745 4689 13

to

account

date

date	details	debit	credit	balance

AMOUNT NOW DUE	

STATEMENT

COMPUSUPPLY LIMITED

Unit 17 Elgar Estate, Broadfield, BR7 4ER
Tel 01908 765756 Fax 01908 765777 Email rob@compusupply.u-net.com
VAT Reg GB 0745 4689 13

to

account

date

date	details	debit	credit	balance

	AMOUNT NOW DUE	

STATEMENT

COMPUSUPPLY LIMITED

Unit 17 Elgar Estate, Broadfield, BR7 4ER
Tel 01908 765756 Fax 01908 765777 Email rob@compusupply.u-net.com
VAT Reg GB 0745 4689 13

to

account

date

date	details	debit	credit	balance

AMOUNT NOW DUE	

3 ACCOUNTING FOR CREDIT SALES AND SALES RETURNS

3.1 Which one of the following is a prime document?

(a)   sales day book

(b)   statement of account sent to T Smith, a debtor

(c)   sales invoice

(d)   sales account

Answer (a) or (b) or (c) or (d)

3.2 Which one of the following is entered in the sales returns day book?

(a)   sales invoice

(b)   pro-forma invoice

(c)   statement of account sent to T Smith, a debtor

(d)   credit note issued

Answer (a) or (b) or (c) or (d)

3.3 Define the following:

•   prime document

•   book of prime entry

•   double-entry book-keeping

•   account

•   ledger

In the Activities which follow, the rate of Value Added Tax is to be calculated at the current rate (17.5% at the time of writing). When calculating VAT amounts, you should ignore fractions of a penny, ie round down to a whole penny.

For Activities 3.4 and 3.5 use a cross-referencing system incorporating the following:

• sales day book	– SDB 55		Teme Sports Ltd	– account no 178
sales returns day book	– SRDB 10		Wyvern Stores	– account no 195
• sales ledger account numbers			• main ledger account numbers	
Dines Stores	– account no 86		sales account	– account no 4001
Meadow Golf Club	– account no 135		sales returns account	– account no 4010
Raven Retailers Ltd	– account no 170		Value Added Tax account	– account no 2200

3.4 Pensax Products Limited manufactures plastic goods which are sold direct to shops. During November 2007 the following credit transactions took place:

2007

3 Nov   Sold goods to Dines Stores £265 + VAT, invoice no 3592

5 Nov   Sold goods to Raven Retailers Limited, £335 + VAT, invoice no 3593

6 Nov   Sold goods to Meadow Golf Club £175 + VAT, invoice no 3594

10 Nov   Sold goods to Wyvern Stores £455 + VAT, invoice no 3595

11 Nov   Sold goods to Dines Stores £290 + VAT, invoice no 3596

13 Nov   Sold goods to Teme Sports Limited £315 + VAT, invoice no 3597

17 Nov   Sold goods to Raven Retailers Limited £1,120 + VAT, invoice no 3598

19 Nov   Sold goods to Teme Sports Limited £825 + VAT, invoice no 3599

21 Nov   Sold goods to Dines Stores £354 + VAT, invoice no 3600

24 Nov   Sold goods to Meadow Golf Club £248 + VAT, invoice no 3601

27 Nov   Sold goods to Wyvern Stores £523 + VAT, invoice no 3602

28 Nov   Sold goods to Raven Retailers Limited £187 + VAT, invoice no 3603

You are to:

(a)   enter the above transactions in Pensax Products' sales day book for November 2007

(b)   record the accounting entries in Pensax Products' sales ledger and main ledger

3.5 The following details are the sales returns for Pensax Products for November 2007. They are to be:

(a)   entered in the sales returns day book for November 2007

(b)   recorded in the sales ledger and main ledger (use the ledgers already prepared in the answer to Activity 3.4)

2007

10 Nov   Dines Stores returns goods £55 + VAT, credit note no CN 831 is issued

14 Nov   Wyvern Stores returns goods £60 + VAT, credit note no CN 832 is issued

19 Nov   Meadow Golf Club returns goods £46 + VAT, credit note no CN 833 is issued

24 Nov   Teme Sports Limited returns goods £127 + VAT, credit note no CN 834 is issued

28 Nov   Dines Stores returns goods £87 + VAT, credit note no CN 835 is issued

3.6   John Green runs a wholesale nursery where he grows plants, shrubs and trees. These are sold on credit to garden centres, shops, and local authorities. His book-keeper records sales in an analysed sales day book including columns for total, VAT, net, plants, shrubs, trees. During April 2007 the following credit transactions took place:

2007

2 Apr	Sold trees to Wyvern Council £550 + VAT, invoice no 2741
4 Apr	Sold plants to Mereford Garden Centre £345 + VAT, invoice no 2742
7 Apr	Sold trees £155 and shrubs £265 (both + VAT) to JJ Gardening Services, invoice no 2743
10 Apr	Sold shrubs to Mereford Garden Centre, £275 + VAT, invoice no 2744
11 Apr	Sold plants to Dines Stores £127 + VAT, invoice no 2745
15 Apr	Sold shrubs £127 and plants £352 (both + VAT) to Wyvern Council, invoice no 2746
17 Apr	Sold plants to Harford Post Office £228 + VAT, invoice no 2247
23 Apr	Sold trees to Mereford Garden Centre £175 + VAT, invoice no 2748
25 Apr	Sold plants to Bourne Supplies £155 + VAT, invoice no 2749
29 Apr	Sold trees £265 and plants £451 (both + VAT) to Mereford Garden Centre, invoice no 2750

You are to:

(a)   enter the above transactions into page 76 of the *analysed* sales day book of John Green

(b)   total the day book at 30 April 2007

Notes:

* folio entries are *not* required

* entries in the sales ledger and main ledger are *not* required

4 BALANCING ACCOUNTS AND CONTROL ACCOUNT FOR SALES

4.1 Balance the following accounts at 30 June 2007, bringing down the balances on 1 July:

Dr	Sales Account		Cr
2007	£	2007	£
		1 Jun Balance b/d	17,351
		30 Jun Sales Day Book	3,960

Dr	Sales Returns Account		Cr
2007	£	2007	£
1 Jun Balance b/d	1,084		
30 Jun Sales Returns Day Book	320		

Dr	Value Added Tax Account		Cr
2007	£	2007	£
30 Jun Sales Returns Day Book	56	1 Jun Balance b/d	1,826
		30 Jun Sales Day Book	693

Dr	N Sharma		Cr
2007	£	2007	£
1 Jun Balance b/d	1,495	8 Jun Sales Returns	141
7 Jun Sales	422		
10 Jun Sales	384		
15 Jun Sales	697		

Dr	Nazir & Company		Cr
2007	£	2007	£
1 Jun Balance b/d	863	4 Jun Sales Returns	47
9 Jun Sales	279	19 Jun Sales Returns	94
18 Jun Sales	186		

4.2   You have the following information:

		£
•	opening debtor balances at start of month	12,250
•	credit sales for month	7,390
•	sales returns for month	450
•	cash/cheques received from debtors for month	6,910

What is the figure for closing debtor balances at the end of the month?

(a)   £12,280

(b)   £13,180

(c)   £12,220

(d)   £11,320

Answer (a) or (b) or (c) or (d)

4.3   Would the following errors cause a difference between the balance of the sales ledger control account and the total of the balances in the subsidiary (sales) ledger?

(a)   The sales day book was overcast (overadded) by £100.

(b)   The amount of a sales invoice was debited to the account of Wyvern Traders instead of Wyvern Tiling.

(c)   An invoice for £54 was recorded in the sales day book as £45.

4.4   Prepare a sales ledger control account for the month of April 2007 from the following information:

2007		£
1 Apr	Debit balance brought down	16,395
30 Apr	Credit sales for month	18,647
	Sales returns	2,804
	Cash/cheques received from debtors	21,086

Balance the account at 30 April 2007.

4.5   The main ledger of Mereford Supplies contains the following accounts on 1 November 2007:

sales	balance £24,685.39 credit
sales returns	balance £2,146.83 debit
Value Added Tax	balance £1,086.30 credit

The subsidiary (sales) ledger contains the following accounts on 1 November 2007:

Burton and Company	balance £1,472.41 debit
Haig and Sons	balance £462.28 debit
Norton Traders	balance £392.48 debit
Shipley Limited	balance £68.87 debit
Yarnold Limited	balance £976.18 debit

The following transactions, which have been authorised by the accounts supervisor, took place during November 2007:

4 Nov	Sold goods on credit to Burton and Company £542.51 + VAT, invoice no 7349
6 Nov	Sold goods on credit to Haigh and Sons £368.29 + VAT, invoice no 7350
11 Nov	Norton Traders returned goods £68.59 + VAT, credit note no CN 547 issued
14 Nov	Sold goods on credit to Yarnold Limited £241.76 + VAT, invoice no 7351
16 Nov	Sold goods on credit to Norton Traders £393.43 + VAT, invoice no 7352
17 Nov	Sold goods on credit to Shipley Limited £627.95 + VAT, invoice no 7353
20 Nov	Yarnold Limited returned goods £110.55 + VAT, credit note no CN 548 issued
24 Nov	Sold goods on credit to Burton and Company £197.52 + VAT, invoice no 7354
25 Nov	Sold goods on credit to Haigh and Sons £315.69 + VAT, invoice no 7355
29 Nov	Shipley Limited returned goods £107.46 + VAT, credit note no CN 549 issued

You are to:

(a)   prepare the accounts in the main ledger – including a sales ledger control account – and subsidiary (sales) ledger of Mereford Supplies and record the balances at 1 November 2007

(b)   enter the above transactions in Mereford Supplies' sales day book and sales returns day book for November 2007

(c)   from the books of prime entry, record the accounting entries in the main ledger and subsidiary (sales) ledger, balancing all accounts at the month-end (30 November 2007)

(d)   reconcile the control account balance with the subsidiary accounts at 1 November and 30 November 2007

5 RECEIVING AND RECORDING PAYMENTS

5.1 You are operating a cash till at the firm where you work. Today the cash float at the start of the day is £22.30, made up as follows:

2 x £5 notes	=	£10.00
6 x £1 coins	=	£6.00
6 x 50p coins	=	£3.00
8 x 20p coins	=	£1.60
10 x 10p coins	=	£1.00
8 x 5p coins	=	£0.40
12 x 2p coins	=	£0.24
6 x 1p coins	=	£0.06
		£22.30

The following are the sales which pass through the till today:

		Amount of sales £	Notes and/or coin tendered
Customer	1	7.50	£10 note
	2	3.38	£5 note
	3	2.29	two £1 coins and a 50p coin
	4	18.90	£20 note
	5	6.04	£10 note, £1 coin, two 2p coins
	6	26.36	three £10 notes
	7	4.30	four £1 coins and a 50p coin

You are to:

(a) state the amount of change to be given to each customer

(b) state the notes and/or coin that will be given in change, using the minimum number possible

(c) calculate the denominations of notes and coin that will remain in the till at the end of the day

(d)   retain a cash float which does not exceed £30.00 (show the denominations of notes and coin); the remainder of the cash is to be banked (show denominations)

(e)   prepare a summary of the day's transactions in the following form:

		£
	cash float at start	22.30
plus	sales made during the day	———
equals	amount of cash held at end of day	
less	cash float retained for next day	———
	amount banked	═══

5.2   You work as an accounts assistant in the Accounts Department of Mercia Pumps Ltd, Unit 13, Severn Trading Estate, Mereford MR3 4GF.   Today is 3 April 2007.   In the morning's post are a number of cheques enclosed with remittance advices. These cheques are illustrated below.

Examine the cheques carefully, and identify any problems, and state what action (if any) you will take, and why. Draft letters where appropriate for your Manager's (Mrs D Strong) signature.

You note from your records that the addresses are as follows:

(a)   The Accounts Department, A & S Systems, 5 High Street, Mereford MR1 2JF

(b)   Mrs P Thorne, Hillside Cottage, Mintfield, MR4 9HG

(c)   The Accounts Department, C Darwin Ltd, 89 Baker Street, Mereford MR2 6RG

(d)   Mr I M King, 56 Beaconsfield Drive, Pershore MR7 5GF

(a)

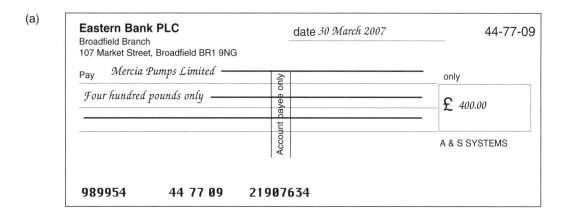

(b)

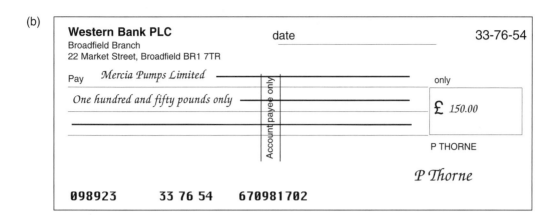

Western Bank PLC
Broadfield Branch
22 Market Street, Broadfield BR1 7TR

date _____

33-76-54

Pay *Mercia Pumps Limited* _____ only

One hundred and fifty pounds only _____

£ *150.00*

Account payee only

P THORNE

P Thorne

098923   33 76 54   670981702

(c)

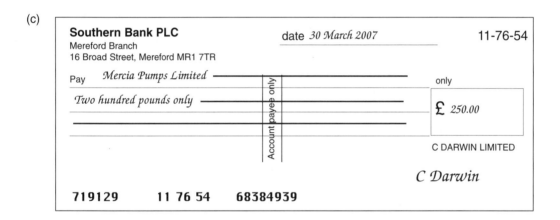

Southern Bank PLC
Mereford Branch
16 Broad Street, Mereford MR1 7TR

date *30 March 2007*

11-76-54

Pay *Mercia Pumps Limited* _____ only

Two hundred pounds only _____

£ *250.00*

Account payee only

C DARWIN LIMITED

C Darwin

719129   11 76 54   68384939

(d)

Mr King has made the cheque payable to your Sales Director, John Hopkins.

Northern Bank PLC
Mereford Branch
28 High Street, Mereford MR1 8FD

date *30 March 2007*

22-01-59

Pay *John Hopkins* _____ only

Sixty pounds only _____

£ *60.00*

Account payee only

I KING

I M King

123456   22 01 59   37537147

5.3 You work as a cashier at Cripplegate DIY store. The date today is January 20 2007. You deal with a number of customers who wish to make payment using cheques and cheque card. What action would you take in the following circumstances, and why?

(a) Card limit £100, expiry June 2007, code 11-76-54. The name on the card is J E Drew. The lady explains that she has just got married, and Drew is her maiden name.

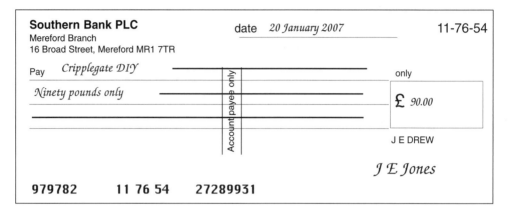

(b) Card limit £100, expiry May 2007, code 22-01-59. Mr King wants to buy some garden furniture costing £150.95. He has made out the following cheques in advance.

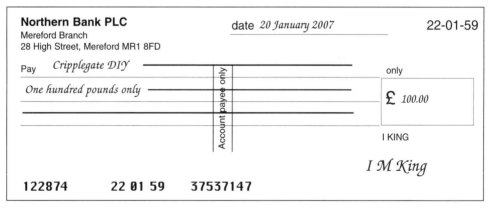

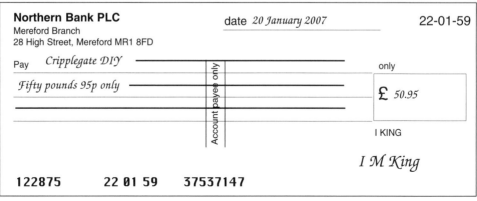

(c)   Card limit £200, expiry April 2007, code 33-76-54. The cheque card is handed to you in a plastic wallet and the signature on the card does not quite tally with the signature on the cheque. The customer says that he has sprained his wrist and this has affected his writing.

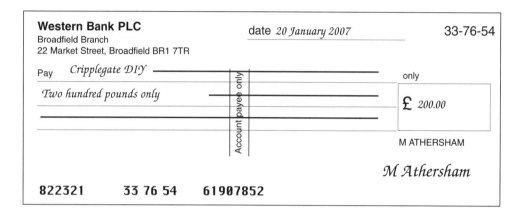

(d)   Card limit £200, expiry August 2007, code 88-76-54. Mrs Blackstone is in a great hurry and asks you to be as quick as you can. She seems to be rather agitated. The signature on the cheque matches the signature on the card and everything else seems to be in order.

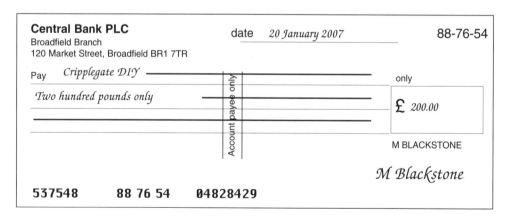

6 PAYING INTO THE BANK

6.1 You are working in the accounts department of Martley Fruits Limited, Maytree Farm, Martley MR7 2LX. Part of your job is to deal with the cheques received in the post, and to prepare those cheques for banking. During the course of a working day you deal with a number of cheques, some of which may cause problems. Your supervisor, Mark Tucker, asks you to identify the problems, and state in each case how you would deal with them. Write down your answers using the schedule on the next page.

	customer	amount	comments
(a)	Henry Young & Co	£1,245	you need to find out whether this cheque is to be paid before you can despatch the goods – rapid clearance is required
(b)	Ivor Longway	£342.90	the date on the cheque is three months old
(c)	Ned Morgan	£837.89	the date on the cheque is ten months old
(d)	Lisa Jones	£90.00	you receive this cheque from the bank; the cheque is marked 'Post dated'; on inspecting the cheque you see that the cheque is dated three months in the future
(e)	N Patel	£78.00	you receive this cheque from the bank; it is marked 'Payment Countermanded by order of Drawer'
(f)	N Trebbiano	£78.98	there is no crossing on the cheque

When you have checked your answer schedule with your tutor you are to draft appropriate letters for your supervisor's signature to the following customers (use today's date):

Ned Morgan, 72 Malvern Crescent, Milton Park, MR6 2CS

Lisa Jones, c/o The Kings Arms, Leatherton, MR6 9SD

customer	problem	solution
Henry Young & Co		
Ivor Longway		
Ned Morgan		
Lisa Jones		
N Patel		
N Trebbiano		

6.2 A colleague, Lisa, who works in the Accounts Department of Wyvern (Office Products) Limited has been handed the latest bank statement by your supervisor, Alfred Hunter. Lisa, who is new to the job, has two queries:

- a credit on 2 April appears as £485.02; your paying slip copy shows the total as £485.04.

- Lisa says she cannot find a paying-in slip copy for the £1,500 received on 4 April

The documentation you have available is shown below.

NATIONAL BANK PLC

Statement of Account

Branch: Mereford

Account: Wyvern (Office Products) Ltd
Account no 01099124   Sheet no 105   Statement date 10 Apr 2007

Date	Details	Withdrawals	Deposits	Balance
2007		£	£	£
1 Apr	Balance brought forward			1,300.00 Cr
1 Apr	Credit		2,000.00	3,300.00 Cr
1 Apr	BACS Prime Hotels Ltd		2,000.00	5,300.00 Cr
2 Apr	Credit		485.02	5,785.02 Cr
3 Apr	Bank charges	70.00		5,715.02 Cr
4 Apr	NationalNet webshop sales		1,500.00	7,215.02 Cr
10 Apr	Cheque 123745	1,860.00		5,355.02 Cr

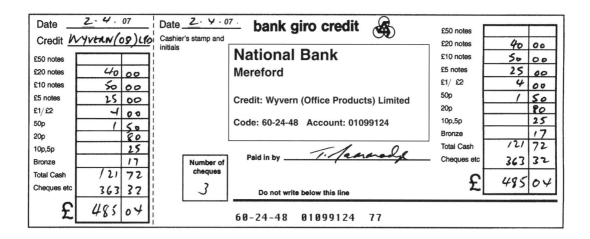

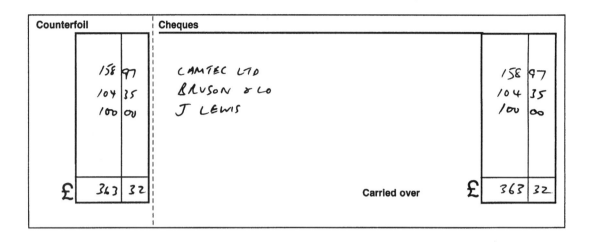

REMITTANCE ADVICE
BRUSON & CO
25 Melody Chambers, Gloucester GL1 2RF
Tel 01452 37232182 Fax 01452 37234496

Wyvern (Office Products) Ltd
12 Lower Hyde Street
Mereford MR1 2JF

Cheque No	774474
Date	18 February 2007
Account	2947

date	our ref.	your ref.	amount	discount	payment
16.3.03	8274	35357	104.33	00.00	104.33

cheque value	£ 104.33

NATIONALNET WEBSHOP SALES – PAYMENT ADVICE

Customer Wyvern (Office Products) Ltd

Item Website Sales to 1 April

Amount £1,500.00

Payment BACS payment to account 01099124 at 60 24 48 on 4 April 2007

You are to

(a) Explain to Lisa what has happened in relation to the paying-in slip dated 1 April and the bank statement.

(b) Write down in numbered points what actions you think should be taken as a result of the mistake on the credit.

(c) Explain to Lisa what the bank statement entry on 4 April represents.

7 CASH BOOK – RECORDING RECEIPTS

7.1 The discount allowed column of the cash book is totalled at regular intervals and transferred to:

(a)   the credit side of discount allowed account

(b)   the debit side of discount allowed account

(c)   the debit side of sales account

(d)   the credit side of sales account

Answer (a) or (b) or (c) or (d)

7.2 The VAT column on the receipts side of the cash book is totalled at regular intervals and transferred to:

(a)   the debit side of sales returns account

(b)   the debit side of VAT account

(c)   the credit side of sales account

(d)   the credit side of VAT account

Answer (a) or (b) or (c) or (d)

7.3 The following are the receipts transactions of Marcle Enterprises for October 2007:

1 Oct	Balances from previous month: cash £280, bank £2,240
4 Oct	Received a cheque from a debtor, M Perry Limited, £475
5 Oct	Cash sales of £240 + VAT, received in cash
11 Oct	Received a BACS advice for £1,295 from T Francis Limited in full settlement of their account of £1,305
15 Oct	Cash sales of £320 + VAT, received in cash
17 Oct	Received a cheque for £640 from H Watson, in full settlement of her account of £660
18 Oct	Received a loan of £1,000 from the bank (no VAT)
22 Oct	Cash sales of £480 + VAT, received half in cash, and half by cheque
24 Oct	Rent received from tenant, £150 in cash (no VAT)
30 Oct	Received a cheque for £464 from M Perry Limited in full settlement of their account of £480

The rate of Value Added Tax is 17.5%

All cheques are banked on the day of receipt

Account numbers are to be used – see next page

You are to:

- Enter the above receipts on page 67 of the three column cash book of Marcle Enterprises.

- Sub-total the money columns at 31 October.

- Show the entries to be made in the following accounts:

  subsidiary (sales) ledger
  T Francis Limited (account no 445)
  M Perry Limited (account no 675)
  H Watson (account no 840)

  main ledger
  sales ledger control account (account no 6001)
  discount allowed account (account no 6501)
  bank loan (account no 2210)
  rent received account (account no 4951)
  sales account (account no 4001)
  VAT account (account no 2200)

7.4 The following are the receipts transactions of Kendrick and Company for November 2007:

1 Nov	Balances from previous month: cash £125, bank £1,529
5 Nov	D McNamara, a debtor, settles an invoice for £100, paying £95 in cash and receiving £5 discount for prompt settlement
7 Nov	Cash sales £235 (including Value Added Tax), received by cheque
12 Nov	Rent received from tenant, £200 by cheque (no VAT)
15 Nov	Cash sales of £423 (including Value Added Tax), received by cheque
19 Nov	Received a cheque for £595 from Johnson & Co, a debtor, in full settlement of their account of £610
20 Nov	Cash sales of £94 (including Value Added Tax), received in cash
26 Nov	Received a cheque for £475 from Mendez Limited, in full settlement of their account of £500
28 Nov	Additional capital paid in, £2,500 by cheque (no VAT)

The rate of Value Added Tax is 17.5%

All cheques are banked on the day of receipt

Account numbers are to be used – see next page

You are to:

- Enter the above receipts on page 24 of the cash book of Kendrick and Company, using columns for date, details, folio, discount allowed, VAT, cash and bank.

- Sub-total the money columns at 30 November.

- Show the entries to be made in the following accounts:

subsidiary (sales) ledger

Johnson & Co (account no 355)

D McNamara (account no 460)

Mendez Limited (account no 505)

main ledger

capital account (account no 3005)

sales ledger control account (account no 6001)

discount allowed account (account no 6501)

rent received account (account no 4951)

sales account (account no 4001)

VAT account (account no 2200)

7.5 Martin Peters runs a building supplies company. He buys in bulk from manufacturers and sells in smaller quantities to trade customers on credit and to the public on cash terms. His business is registered for VAT.

He uses a cash book which analyses receipts between:

- discount allowed
- VAT
- cash sales
- subsidiary (sales) ledger
- rent received

The following transactions take place during the week commencing 19 November 2007:

19 Nov	Balances from previous week: cash £384.21, bank £2,576.80
19 Nov	Cash sales of £354.25 (including VAT), cheques received
20 Nov	Received a BACS advice for £678.11 from Barbourne Builders in full settlement of their account of £695.50
20 Nov	Cash sales of £254.88 (including VAT), cash received
21 Nov	Rent received from a tenant of part of the premises, £285.75 by cheque (no VAT)
21 Nov	Cash sales of £476.29 (including VAT), cheques received
22 Nov	Rent received from another tenant, £325.00 in cash (no VAT)
22 Nov	Cash sales of £351.48 (including VAT), cash received
23 Nov	A debtor, J Johnson, settles an invoice for £398.01, paying £389.51 by BACS, £8.50 discount being allowed for prompt settlement
23 Nov	Cash sales of £487.29 (including VAT), cheques received
23 Nov	A debtor, Wyvern Council settles an invoice for £269.24 by cheque

The rate of Value Added Tax is 17.5%

All cheques are banked on the day of receipt

Account numbers are to be used as follows:

Main ledger account codes (extract):	
1000	Cash book
2000	Sales ledger control
3000	Discount allowed
4000	Sales
5000	Rent received
6000	VAT

Subsidiary (sales) ledger account codes (extract):	
110	Barbourne Builders
440	J Johnson
930	Wyvern Council

Using the layouts on the next three pages, you are to:

• Enter the above receipts on page 45 of the analysed cash book of Martin Peters (VAT amounts should be rounded down to the nearest penny).

• Total the money columns at 23 November.

• Show the entries to be made in the main ledger and the subsidiary (sales) ledger.

ACCOUNT NO 1000 CASH BOOK (RECEIPTS)

CBR 45

Date 2007	Details	Reference	Cash £	Bank £	Discount allowed £	VAT £	Cash sales £	Subsidiary (sales) ledger £	Rent received £	Subsidiary (sales) ledger code
Main ledger codes	DR									
	CR									

MAIN LEDGER

2000 Sales Ledger Control							
Date	Details	Folio	Amount	Date	Details	Folio	Amount
2007			£	2007			£

3000 Discount Allowed							
Date	Details	Folio	Amount	Date	Details	Folio	Amount
2007			£	2007			£

4000 Sales							
Date	Details	Folio	Amount	Date	Details	Folio	Amount
2007			£	2007			£

5000 Rent Received							
Date	Details	Folio	Amount	Date	Details	Folio	Amount
2007			£	2007			£

MAIN LEDGER

			6000 VAT				
Date	Details	Folio	Amount	Date	Details	Folio	Amount
2007			£	2007			£

SUBSIDIARY (SALES) LEDGER

			110 Barbourne Builders				
Date	Details	Folio	Amount	Date	Details	Folio	Amount
2007			£	2007			£

			440 J Johnson				
Date	Details	Folio	Amount	Date	Details	Folio	Amount
2007			£	2007			£

			930 Wyvern Council				
Date	Details	Folio	Amount	Date	Details	Folio	Amount
2007			£	2007			£

9 DOCUMENTS FOR GOODS AND SERVICES RECEIVED

9.1 You have just started work as an accounts assistant in the purchasing department of Litho Printers. Your supervisor has asked you to buy 150 reams (a ream is 500 sheets) of standard quality white A4 copy paper. He said "shop around if you can – prices can vary a lot."

You have telephoned four different stationery suppliers for their stationery catalogues and have made enquiries about special offers on copy paper. The best deals seem to be from Saxon Supplies. An extract from their catalogue (which they have faxed through) is shown below.

SAXON SUPPLIES

Unit 12 Hereward Industrial Estate, Warborough, WA3 5TG

Tel 01807 282482 Fax 01807 282412 Email JJ@Saxon.u-net-com.uk

BARGAINS OF THE MONTH!

reference	product	unit	list price (VAT excl)	sale price (VAT excl)
RCA4	A4 Roxo 80gsm copy paper (white only) standard quality	ream	3.49	2.79
REFA4	A4 Roxo 80gsm copy paper (white – extra fine quality)	ream	4.99	3.49
RLA4	A4 Roxo 80gsm laser paper	ream	5.49	4.99
CCA4	Colour 80gsm copy paper Add code to your order ref: R (red) B (blue) Y (yellow)	ream	5.50	4.50
EWDLP	White self-seal DL envelopes (plain)	1000 box	25.00	10.99
EWDLSS	White self-seal DL envelopes (window)	1000 box	35.00	16.99
N1	'Nifty' air bubble mail envelopes 200mm x 300mm	100 box	22.00	18.00
N2	'Nifty' air bubble mail envelopes 235mm x 370mm	100 box	25.00	21.00
FR15	Fax roll 210mm x 15m	roll	2.85	1.50
FR30	Fax roll 216mm x 30m	roll	5.00	3.50

Your supervisor, who has seen the Saxon Supplies prices, says that she also wants to order 50 fax rolls (30m) and 5 boxes of white self-seal DL window envelopes which are used to send out customer statements.

You are to complete the purchase order shown below for the 150 reams of ordinary white copy paper and the extra items requested by the supervisor. You are authorised to sign the order (use your own name). Saxon Supplies has said over the telephone that you can have an initial 15% discount on all orders. The purchase order number is 2892. The date is 8 December 2007.

PURCHASE ORDER	**litho printers**
	Unit 7 Buttermere Estate
	Station Road
	Broadfield
	BR6 3TR
	Tel 01908 456291 Fax 01908 456913

to

purchase order no

date

product code	quantity	description

Authorised   signature...date....................................

9.2   Later in the morning you have to check a delivery note for goods just received against the original purchase order (see page 46). Write a letter to the supplier (see page 47) explaining what is wrong with the delivery. Use your own name and the title 'Accounts Assistant'. The date is 8 December 2007.

PURCHASE ORDER

litho printers

Unit 7 Buttermere Estate
Station Road
Broadfield
BR6 3TR
Tel 01908 456291 Fax 01908 456913

to

Eleco Supplies
79 Broadacre
Boreham
BO7 6TG

purchase order no   3601

date   20 November 2007

product code	quantity	description
23477C	5	Typo office chairs, charcoal

Authorised   signature...... *A Morello* ....date... *20.11.07* ....

DELIVERY NOTE

eleco supplies

79 Broadacre
Boreham
BO7 6TG
Tel 01208 070111 Fax 01208 070149

to

Litho Printers Limited
Unit 7 Buttermere Estate
Station Road
Broadfield
BR6 3TR

Delivery Note No   39823
Purchase Order no   3601
Date   5 December 2007
Delivery   Lightning Carriers

product code	quantity	description
22477C	5	Executive chairs, charcoal

Received in good condition

signature...... *R Smithers* ....date... *8.12.07* ....

litho printers

Unit 7 Buttermere Estate, Station Road,
Broadfield BR6 3TR
Tel 01908 456291 Fax 01908 456913
E-mail ben@litho.u-net.com

Litho Printers Limited. Registered office: Unit 7 Buttermere Estate, Station Road, Broadfield BR6 3TR
Registered in England No 3539857. VAT Reg GB 32 73687 78

9.3   After lunch on the same day (8 December 2007) you have to check three incoming invoices against the appropriate goods received notes which have been raised (see pages 48 to 50). They should be checked for accuracy and to make sure that they apply to the goods supplied. You are to make a list of any errors or discrepancies and pass it to your supervisor on the schedule on page 51. Each of the suppliers normally gives 20% trade discount, but no cash discount.

INVOICE

JUMBO STATIONERY

91 HIGH STREET, BROADFIELD, BR7 4ER
Tel 01908 129426 Fax 01908 129919

invoice to

Litho Printers Limited
Unit 7 Buttermere Estate
Station Road
Broadfield BR6 3TR

invoice no	234672
account	2984
your reference	3627
date/tax point	1 December 2007

product code	description	quantity	price	unit	total	discount %	net
JB234	Jetstream Biros, finepoint, black	20	2.25	box	45.00	10	40.50

terms	goods total	40.50
Net monthly	VAT	7.08
Carriage paid		
E & OE	TOTAL	47.58

JAVELIN OFFICE MACHINES   *invoice*

Unit 19 Elgar Estate, Broadfield, BR7 4ER
Tel 01908 765101 Fax 01908 765304

invoice to

Litho Printers Limited
Unit 7 Buttermere Estate
Station Road
Broadfield BR6 3TR

invoice no	10483
account	935
order reference	3629
date/tax point	2 December 2007

product code	description	quantity	price	unit	total	discount %	net
M17C	Multipoint 17" colour monitor	1	499.00	item	499.00	20	399.20

terms	goods total	399.20
Net monthly	VAT	69.86
Carriage paid		
E & OE	TOTAL	469.06

EDWARD HUGHES LIMITED

invoice

Unit 3 Bronglais Estate, Pwllmadoc, LL1 4ER
Tel 01708 323242 Fax 01708 323242 VAT Reg GB 5019 46 2

invoice to

Litho Printers Limited
Unit 7 Buttermere Estate
Station Road
Broadfield BR6 3TR

invoice no	12931
account	9742
your reference	3628
date/tax point	2 December 2007

product code	description	quantity	price	unit	total	discount %	net
3883	Automatic offset crimper	1	8295.00	unit	8295.00	20	6636.00

terms

Net monthly
Carriage paid
E & OE

goods total	6636.00
VAT	1116.30
TOTAL	7752.30

---

litho printers

GOODS RECEIVED NOTE

GRN no.	301
supplier	Jumbo Stationery
date	3 December 2007

order ref.	quantity	description
3627	15 boxes	Jetstream biros (fine point, black)

received by *R Nixon* .... checked by *I Singh* ....

condition of goods good 15 boxes

damages

shortages 5 boxes

---

litho printers   GOODS RECEIVED NOTE

GRN no.   303

supplier   Javelin Office Machines

date   4 December 2007

order ref.	quantity	description
3629	1	Multipoint 17 inch colour monitor

received by.....*J Kennedy*.........................checked by.........*I Singh*...........

condition of goods   good √

damages

shortages

---

litho printers   GOODS RECEIVED NOTE

GRN no.   302

supplier   Edward Hughes Ltd

date   4 December 2007

order ref.	quantity	description
3628	1	Automatic offset crimper

received by.....*J Kennedy*.........................checked by.........*M Jones*...........

condition of goods   good   √

damages

shortages

date	Order no.	Action to be taken

9.4 Today it is 12 December 2007 and the stationery order from Saxon Supplies (see Task 9.1) has arrived. The goods received note shows that the correct quantity of goods has been received and that there are no wrong goods or damaged items.

You have now been passed the invoice for checking against the original order (produced in Task 9.1). If there are any problems with the invoice, write them down on the memorandum on the next page. Address the memo to your supervisor, James Ridelle. Use your own name. Your title is Accounts Assistant.

INVOICE

SAXON SUPPLIES

Unit 12 Hereward Industrial Estate, Warborough, WA3 5TG
Tel 01807 282482 Fax 01807 282412 Email JJ@Saxon.u-net-com.uk

invoice to

| Litho Printers Limited |
| Unit 7 Buttermere Estate |
| Station Road |
| Broadfield BR6 3TR |

invoice no	89422
account	230
your reference	2892
date/tax point	10 December 2007

product code	description	quantity	price	unit	total	discount %	net
RCA4	A4 Roxo 80gsm copy paper	150	3.49	ream	523.50	15	444.98
FR30	Fax roll 216mm x 30mm	50	3.50	unit	175.00	15	148.75
EWDLSS	White self-seal window DL envelopes	5	16.99	box	84.95	15	72.21

terms
Net monthly
Carriage paid
E & OE

goods total	665.94
VAT	116.53
TOTAL	782.47

MEMORANDUM

date
to
from
subject

9.5 You work for H Patel & Co, a wholesaler. You are an accounts assistant and one of your tasks is to process payments to suppliers. The business normally pays on the 7th and 21st day of each month (or the next working day). The company takes full advantage of the credit terms offered by its suppliers.

H Patel & Co has recently been having problems with its supplier ABC Import Agency, which supplies on 30 day terms. Orders have been delivered late and wrong goods have been supplied. As a result H Patel & Co withheld the August payment until a credit note for £470.00 was received in respect of wrong goods supplied.

The credit note finally arrived on 25 September 2007.

It is 7 October and you have been told that you can now process a payment to ABC Import Agency. The statement is shown below.

You are to calculate the amount owing and complete the remittance advice and cheque shown on the next page. You will not sign the cheque, as it has to be authorised and signed by Hitten Patel.

STATEMENT OF ACCOUNT

ABC Import Agency
30 Eastway Road
Manchester
M1 2RB
Tel 01601 764098 Fax 01601 764083 Email mail@abcimportco.com
VAT Reg GB 0748 4872 23

TO

| H Patel & Co |
| 76 Dockside Road |
| Deeford |
| DE1 8AS |

account **3945**

date **30 September 2007**

date	details	debit £	credit £	balance £
2007				
1 Sep	Balance b/f			5,600.00
3 Sep	Invoice 13621	1,400.00		7,000.00
12 Sep	Invoice 13688	1,665.00		8,665.00
22 Sep	Invoice 13721	2,991.00		11,656.00
25 Sep	Credit note 744		470.00	11,186.00
			TOTAL	**£ 11,186.00**

REMITTANCE ADVICE

TO

FROM

H Patel & Co
76 Dockside Road
Deeford
DE1 8AS
Tel 01324 8752946 Fax 01324 8752955
VAT REG GB 0745 8383 77

Account: **Date:**

date	your reference	our reference	payment amount

CHEQUE TOTAL

Southern Bank PLC
Deeford Branch
22 Water Street, Deeford DE1 7TR

date _____   97-76-44

Pay _____

_____   only

Account payee only

£

H PATEL & CO

234871   97 76 44   23992211

10 ACCOUNTING FOR CREDIT PURCHASES AND PURCHASES RETURNS

10.1 Which one shows the correct accounting entries to record the purchase of goods for resale on credit?

	Debit	**Credit**
(a)	purchases returns account	supplier's account
(b)	purchases account	supplier's account
(c)	supplier's account	purchases returns account
(d)	supplier's account	purchases account

Answer (a) or (b) or (c) or (d)

In the Activities which follow, the rate of Value Added Tax is to be calculated at the current rate (17.5% at the time of writing). When calculating VAT amounts, you should ignore fractions of a penny, ie round down to a whole penny.

For Activities 10.2 and 10.3 use a cross-referencing system incorporating the following:

purchases day book	– PDB 36
purchases returns day book	– PRDB 11

purchases ledger account numbers

S Burston	– account no 530
Iley Wholesalers	– account no 605
Malvern Manufacturing	– account no 625
SG Enterprises	– account no 720

main ledger accounts

purchases account	– account no 5001
purchases returns account	– account no 5010
Value Added Tax account	– account no 2200

10.2 During July 2007, Tyax Trading Company had the following credit transactions:

2007

3 Jul	Bought goods from Malvern Manufacturing £170 + VAT, invoice no 7321
9 Jul	Bought goods from S Burston £265 + VAT, invoice SB745
12 Jul	Bought goods from Iley Wholesalers £450 + VAT, invoice no 4721
18 Jul	Bought goods from SG Enterprises £825 + VAT, invoice no 3947
23 Jul	Bought goods from S Burston £427 + VAT, invoice no SB773
30 Jul	Bought goods from Malvern Manufacturing £364 + VAT, invoice no 7408

You are to:

(a)   enter the above transactions in Tyax Trading Company's purchases day book for July 2007

(b)   record the accounting entries in Tyax Trading Company's purchases ledger and main ledger

10.3 The following are the purchases returns of Tyax Trading Company for July 2007. They are to be:

(a)   entered in the purchases returns day book for July 2007

(b)   recorded in the purchases ledger and main ledger (use the ledgers already prepared in the answer to Activity 10.2).

2007

11 Jul	Returned goods to Malvern Manufacturing £70 + VAT, credit note no CN345 received
17 Jul	Returned goods to Iley Wholesalers for £85 + VAT, credit note no CN241 received
24 Jul	Returned goods to SG Enterprises for £25 + VAT, credit note no 85 received
31 Jul	Returned goods to S Burston for £55 + VAT, credit note no 295 received

10.4 The Oasis Trading Company records its credit purchases in an analysed day book with the following headings: VAT, net, goods for resale, printing, telephone. The transactions for March 2007 are as follows:

2007

3 Mar	Bought goods for resale from Severn Valley Traders £255.50 + VAT
4 Mar	Bought goods for resale from Mercian Suppliers £356.25 + VAT
6 Mar	Received an invoice for £136.95 + VAT from Print Services Limited for printing
10 Mar	Bought goods for resale from D James Limited £368.21 + VAT
14 Mar	Received an invoice for £218.25 + VAT from United Telecom for telephone costs

17 Mar   Bought goods for resale from Wyvern Traders £45.40 + VAT

19 Mar   Bought goods for resale from A-Z Traders £496.84 + VAT

21 Mar   Received an invoice for £154.65 + VAT from Saturn Communications for telephone costs

24 Mar   Bought goods for resale from A J Knowles £151.20 + VAT

25 Mar   Bought goods for resale from Severn Valley Traders £357.24 + VAT

28 Mar   Received an invoice for £121.47 + VAT from Total Communications plc for telephone costs

31 Mar   Received an invoice for £117.25 from Print Services Limited for printing

You are to:

(a)   give each invoice a unique number – starting with number 4592

(b)   enter the above transactions into page 45 of the company's analysed purchases day book

(c)   total the day book at 31 March 2007

Note: Entries in the purchases ledger and main ledger are not required.

11 BALANCING ACCOUNTS AND CONTROL ACCOUNT FOR PURCHASES

11.1 Balance the following accounts at 30 April 2007, bringing down the balance on 1 May:

Dr		Purchases Account				Cr
2007			£	2007		£
1 Apr	Balance b/d		33,649			
30 Apr	Purchases Day Book		7,840			

Dr		Purchases Returns Account				Cr
2007			£	2007		£
				1 Apr	Balance b/d	856
				30 Apr	Purchases Returns Day Book	400

Dr		Value Added Tax Account				Cr
2007			£	2007		£
30 Apr	Purchases Day Book		1,372	1 Apr	Balance b/d	1,873
				30 Apr	Purchases Returns Day Book	70

Dr		Shah and Company				Cr
2007			£	2007		£
23 Apr	Purchases Returns		94	1 Apr	Balance b/d	591
				9 Apr	Purchases	783
				22 Apr	Purchases	396
				28 Apr	Purchases	421

Dr		Martinez Limited				Cr
2007			£	2007		£
9 Apr	Purchases Returns		47	1 Apr	Balance b/d	965
17 Apr	Purchases Returns		141	4 Apr	Purchases	187
				20 Apr	Purchases	246
				27 Apr	Purchases	397

11.2 You have the following information:

		£
•	opening creditor balances at start of month	24,795
•	credit purchases for month	15,355
•	purchases returns for month	420
•	cash/cheques paid to creditors for month	14,935

What is the figure for closing creditor balances at the end of the month?

(a)   £15,915

(b)   £25,635

(c)   £24,795

(d)   £23,955

Answer (a) or (b) or (c) or (d)

11.3 Prepare a purchases ledger control account for the month of June 2007 from the following information:

2007		£
1 Jun	Credit balance brought down	27,932
30 Jun	Credit purchases for month	19,354
	Purchases returns	1,083
	Cash/cheques paid to creditors	22,649
	Transfer of credit balances to sales ledger	1,378

The creditors figure at 30 June is to be entered as the balancing figure.

11.4 The main ledger of Pembridge and Company contains the following accounts on 1 August 2007:

purchases	balance £16,241.38 debit
purchases returns	balance £1,854.29 credit
Value Added Tax	balance £1,437.94 credit

The subsidiary (purchases) ledger contains the following accounts on 1 August 2007:

Bakewell Limited	balance £476.81 credit
Edge and Company	balance £1,107.52 credit
M Lister	balance £908.04 credit
Percival and Company	balance £250.49 credit
Trent Supplies	balance £749.25 credit
Vector Metals Limited	balance £397.64 credit

The following transactions, which have been authorised by the accounts supervisor, took place during August 2007 (note that Pembridge and Company gives each invoice and credit note received its own unique number):

2 Aug	Bought goods on credit from Trent Supplies £179.21 + VAT, invoice no 3954
5 Aug	Bought goods on credit from Percival and Company £352.47 + VAT, invoice no 3955
6 Aug	Returned goods to Bakewell Limited £74.38 + VAT, credit note no 768
9 Aug	Bought goods on credit from M Lister £450.68 + VAT, invoice no 3956
12 Aug	Bought goods on credit from Vector Metals Limited £370.27 + VAT, invoice no 3957
14 Aug	Bought goods on credit from Edge and Company £210.48 + VAT, invoice no 3958
17 Aug	Returned goods to Percival and Company £114.36 + VAT, credit note no 769
19 Aug	Bought goods on credit from Trent Supplies £780.36 + VAT, invoice no 3959
25 Aug	Bought goods on credit from M Lister £246.33 + VAT, invoice no 3960
27 Aug	Returned goods to Vector Metals Limited £68.41 + VAT, credit note no 770
29 Aug	Transfer of debit balance of £754.26 in the subsidiary (sales) ledger to Edge and Company's account in the subsidiary (purchases) ledger

You are to:

(a)   prepare the accounts in the main ledger – including a purchases ledger control account – and subsidiary (purchases) ledger of Pembridge and Company and record the balances at 1 August 2007

(b)   enter the above transactions in Pembridge's purchases day book and purchases returns day book for August 2007

(c)   from the books of prime entry, record the accounting entries – including the set-off – in the main ledger and subsidiary (purchases) ledger, balancing all accounts at the month-end (31 August 2007)

(d)   reconcile the control account balance with the subsidiary accounts at 1 August and 31 August 2007

12 MAKING PAYMENTS

12.1 You work as an assistant in the accounts department of A & S Systems Limited, computer consultants. Your job is to pay purchase invoices. Your file contains 12 invoices which have all been approved for payment.

The company writes out cheques in settlement of suppliers' invoices every week. It is company policy to pay strictly according to the terms of the invoice and to take advantage of settlement discounts whenever possible. Today is 27 March 2007.

You have been on holiday for a fortnight and someone else has done your job for the last two weeks. Your line manager suggests you check carefully to make sure your file is brought up to date and all outstanding invoices are settled, as he suspects some may have been overlooked.

You are to select the invoices due for payment and calculate the amount due on those invoices, taking into account any cash discount. A summary of the invoices is shown below.

invoice date	supplier	terms	net £	VAT £	invoice total £
11.02.07	James Smith Ltd	30 days	456.89	79.95	536.84
13.02.07	R Singh	30 days*	1,200.00	204.75	1,404.75
24.02.07	John Hopkins	30 days	230.75	40.38	271.13
24.02.07	Mereford Supplies	60 days	235.00	41.12	276.12
02.03.07	E Ragle Ltd	30 days	345.89	60.53	406.42
23.03.07	Meteor Ltd	30 days*	2,400.00	409.50	2,809.50
16.02.07	Helen Jarvis	30 days	109.00	19.07	128.07
17.02.07	Martley Electronics	60 days	245.00	42.87	287.87
24.03.07	Jones & Co	30 days*	950.00	162.09	1,112.09
20.02.07	J Marvell	30 days	80.95	14.16	95.11
19.02.07	K Nott	60 days	457.50	80.06	537.56
20.03.07	V Williams	30 days	1,250.00	218.75	1,468.75

* These invoices are marked '2.5% settlement discount for payment within 7 days'.

12.2 Complete the cheques shown on this and the next page in settlement of the invoices you have decided to pay. The date today is 27 March 2007. You will not sign the cheques; this will be done by two authorised signatories.

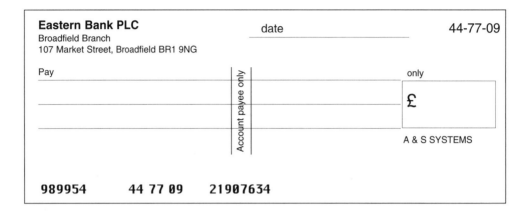

Eastern Bank PLC
Broadfield Branch
107 Market Street, Broadfield BR1 9NG

date _____   44-77-09

Pay _____ only

Account payee only

£ _____

A & S SYSTEMS

989954   44 77 09   21907634

Eastern Bank PLC
Broadfield Branch
107 Market Street, Broadfield BR1 9NG

date _____   44-77-09

Pay _____ only

Account payee only

£ _____

A & S SYSTEMS

989955   44 77 09   21907634

Eastern Bank PLC
Broadfield Branch
107 Market Street, Broadfield BR1 9NG

date _____   44-77-09

Pay _____ only

Account payee only

£ _____

A & S SYSTEMS

989956   44 77 09   21907634

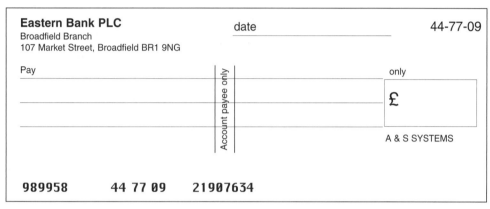

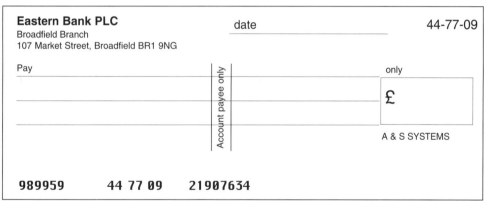

12.3 On 27 March 2007 your supervisor also asks you to arrange three payments: two wage cheques to new employees not yet on the computer payroll and a subscription to a professional organisation. You are to arrange these payments on the documents shown on the next page (you do not need to write out any cheques, or to sign the standing order). The details are as follows:

(a) Wages of £89.00 to R Power at Western Bank, Broadfield, Code 33 76 54, account number 71976234.

(b) Wages of £155.00 to R Patel at Central Bank, Broadfield, Code 88 76 51, account number 04892192.

(c) Monthly subscription of £15.00 (starting 1 April 2007, until further notice) to Association of Software Designers at Eastern Bank, Mereford, 44 77 06, account number 21903461, reference 121092.

Bank Giro Credit 1 — Western Bank plc

Date _____

Credit _____

£50 notes		
£20 notes		
£10 notes		
£5 notes		
£2/£1		
50p		
20p		
10p,5p		
Bronze		
Total Cash		
Cheques etc		
£		

Date _____

Cashier's stamp and initials

Number of cheques

bank giro credit

Western Bank plc

Broadfield

Credit: R Power

Code: 33-76-54   Account: 71976234

Paid in by _____

Do not write below this line

£50 notes		
£20 notes		
£10 notes		
£5 notes		
£2/£1		
50p		
20p		
10p,5p		
Bronze		
Total Cash		
Cheques etc		
£		

Bank Giro Credit 2 — Central Bank PLC

Date _____

Credit _____

£50 notes		
£20 notes		
£10 notes		
£5 notes		
£2/£1		
50p		
20p		
10p,5p		
Bronze		
Total Cash		
Cheques etc		
£		

Date _____

Cashier's stamp and initials

Number of cheques

bank giro credit

Central Bank PLC

Spring Gardens, Broadfield

Credit: R Patel

Code: 88-76-51   Account: 04892192

Paid in by _____

Do not write below this line

£50 notes		
£20 notes		
£10 notes		
£5 notes		
£2/£1		
50p		
20p		
10p,5p		
Bronze		
Total Cash		
Cheques etc		
£		

STANDING ORDER MANDATE

To _____ Bank

Address _____

PLEASE PAY TO

Bank _____ Branch _____ Sort code _____

Beneficiary _____ Account number _____

The sum of **£** _____ Amount in words _____

Date of first payment _____ Frequency of payment _____

Until _____ Reference _____

Account to be debited _____ Account number _____

SIGNATURE(S) ....

.... date..........................

13 PAYROLL PAYMENTS

13.1 Three new staff taken on by Osborne Electronics have been placed on a BACS 'auto credit' system. The details of the staff and the next month's pay are:

employee	payee number	sort code	account no	amount (£)
J Lloyd	456	40 40 40	12826251	786.00
H Thin	457	30 40 50	42447998	899.50
L Bright	458	20 87 65	80975132	885.75

Complete the schedule shown below, ready for signature. The payments should reach the bank accounts on the last working day of next month (based on today's date). The reference is OE3452.

WESTERN BANK PLC
Auto Credit System

Bank branch....Worcester..............................

Customer name...Reference...............................

Date.................................

Sort code	Account no	Name	Payee no	Amount

PAYMENT TOTAL

Please make the above payments to reach the payees on ....(date)

Please debit account no................................with the sum of £...............................

Authorised signature...

13.2 Osborne Electronics has a new member of staff – C Bellamy – on the weekly payroll who is to be paid by cheque for the first week. You are to make out a cheque *ready for signing* (use today's date). The amount is £256.75.

Western Bank PLC	date _____ 75-77-09
Worcester Branch	
44 High Street, Worcester WR1 9NG	
Pay _____	only
_____	£
_____	OSBORNE ELECTRONICS
Account payee only	

574583   75 77 09   79108734

13.3 Delpiero Limited has recorded the following payroll totals for the month of October 2007:

gross pay	£131,300
income tax deducted by PAYE	£26,000
NIC (employees' contribution)	£12,800
NIC (employer's contribution)	£13,200
pension: employer's contribution (non-contributory pension)	£9,750

(a) Calculate the total payroll cost to the employer

(b) Calculate the payment due to the HM Revenue & Customs

(c) Calculate the net pay due to employees

(d) Draw up double-entry accounts for Wages & Salaries, HM Revenue & Customs, Pension Fund, Bank, and Wages & Salaries Control and enter the relevant entries. Assume a nil opening balance for each account. You do not need to balance the accounts

(e) Explain the entries you have made on the following accounts and describe the transactions that they represent:

    (i) bank account

    (ii) HM Revenue & Customs

    (iii) Pension Fund

14 CASH BOOK – RECORDING PAYMENTS

14.1 The discount received column of the cash book is totalled at regular intervals and transferred to:

(a) the debit side of discount received account

(b) the credit side of discount received account

(c) the credit side of general expenses account

(d) the debit side of general expenses account

Answer (a) or (b) or (c) or (d)

14.2 The VAT column on the payments side of the cash book is totalled at regular intervals and transferred to:

(a) the credit side of VAT account

(b) the credit side of sales account

(c) the debit side of VAT account

(d) the debit side of general expenses account

Answer (a) or (b) or (c) or (d)

14.3 You work as the cashier for Middleton Trading Company. A work experience student from the local college is with you today. You show the student the payments side of the cash book with last week's transactions as follows:

Credit			Cash Book: Payments				CBP 36
Date	Details	Folio	Discount received	VAT	Cash	Bank
2007			£	£	£	£
1 Oct	Balance b/d					1,588
1 Oct	Teme Traders	PL				585
2 Oct	Insurance	ML				250
2 Oct	Office stationery	ML		14	94	
3 Oct	Tyax Supplies	PL	10			190
4 Oct	Purchases	ML		21		141
5 Oct	Wages	ML			455	
			10	35	549	2,754

You are to explain to the student what each of the transactions represents and the other accounting entries involved in the transactions. Note that the company's book-keeping system includes a purchases ledger control account.

14.4 The following are the payments transactions of Marcle Enterprises for October 2007:

3 Oct	Cash purchases paid for by cheque, £440 + VAT
5 Oct	Paid Jarvis Supplies a cheque for £625 in full settlement of a debt of £645
8 Oct	Bought office equipment, paying by cheque £320 + VAT
12 Oct	Paid Hallam Limited £237 by cheque
16 Oct	Paid salaries by BACS, £2,247 (no VAT)
18 Oct	Paid telephone expenses by cheque, £329 (including VAT)
22 Oct	Paid T Woods a cheque for £439 in full settlement of a debt of £449
24 Oct	Cash purchases paid for by cheque, £400 + VAT
26 Oct	Paid wages in cash, £420 (no VAT)
29 Oct	The owner of the business withdraws £500 by cheque for own use
30 Oct	Cash purchases paid for in cash, £120 + VAT

The rate of Value Added Tax is 17.5%.

Account numbers are to be used – see below.

You are to:

* Enter the above payments on page 67 of the three column cash book of Marcle Enterprises.

* Sub-total the money columns at 31 October.

* Show the entries to be made in the following accounts:

  subsidiary (purchases) ledger

  Hallam Limited (account no 455)

  Jarvis Supplies (account no 525)

  T Woods (account no 760)

  main ledger

  purchases ledger control account (account no 6002)

  discount received account (account no 6502)

  drawings account (account no 7005)

  office equipment account (account no 750)

  purchases account (account no 5001)

  telephone expenses account (account no 6212)

  VAT account (account no 2200)

  wages and salaries account (account no 7750)

14.5 The following are the payments transactions of Kendrick and Company for November 2007:

5 Nov	Cash purchases paid for by cheque, £235 (including VAT)
7 Nov	Bought office stationery £40 + VAT, paying in cash
9 Nov	Paid a cheque for £355 to Abel and Company, a creditor, in full settlement of an invoice for £370
12 Nov	Cash purchases for £141 (including VAT) paid in cash
13 Nov	Bought office equipment, paying by cheque, £360 + VAT
15 Nov	Paid an invoice for £250 from A Palmer, a creditor, by cheque for £235, £15 being received for prompt settlement
16 Nov	Loan repayment of £250 made to HSCB Bank by direct debit (no VAT)
19 Nov	The owners of the business withdraw £400 by cheque for own use
21 Nov	Cash purchases of £94 (including VAT) paid in cash
26 Nov	Paid a cheque for £325 to P Singh Limited, a creditor, in full settlement of an invoice for £335
27 Nov	Paid salaries by BACS, £1,552 (no VAT)
28 Nov	Cash purchases of £240 + VAT, paid by cheque
29 Nov	Paid wages in cash, £475 (no VAT)
29 Nov	Paid a cheque for £340 to Abel and Company, a creditor, in full settlement of an invoice for £350
30 Nov	Bought office stationery £120 + VAT, paying by cheque

The rate of Value Added Tax is 17.5%
Account numbers are to be used – see below.

You are to:

- Enter the above payments on page 24 of the cash book of Kendrick and Company, using columns for date, details, folio, discount received, VAT, cash and bank.
- Sub-total the money columns at 30 November.
- Show the entries to be made in the following accounts:

  subsidiary (purchases) ledger

  Abel and Company (account no 105)
  A Palmer (account no 495)
  P Singh Limited (account no 645)

  main ledger
  purchases ledger control account (account no 6002)
  discount received account (account no 6502)
  drawings account (account no 7005)
  loan account: HSCB Bank (account no 2250)
  office equipment account (account no 750)
  office stationery account (account no 6384)
  purchases account (account no 5001)
  VAT account (account no 2200)
  wages and salaries account (account no 7750)

14.6 Martin Peters runs a building supplies company. He buys in bulk from manufacturers and sells in smaller quantities to trade customers on credit and to the public on cash terms. His business is registered for VAT.

He uses a cash book which analyses payments between:

- discount received
- VAT
- cash purchases
- subsidiary (purchases) ledger
- wages and salaries
- sundry

The following transactions take place during the week commencing 19 November 2007:

19 Nov	Cash purchases of £150.00 (including VAT) paid by cheque
19 Nov	Paid an invoice for £292.65 from Broughton Brick Company (a creditor) by cheque for £286.40 and receiving £6.25 discount for prompt settlement
20 Nov	Bought stationery £45.50 (including VAT), paying in cash
21 Nov	Paid an invoice for £552.70 from Broad Timber Limited (a creditor) by cheque
21 Nov	Bought central heating oil £124.04 + VAT, paying by cheque
22 Nov	Paid wages £182.31 in cash (no VAT)
23 Nov	Cash purchases of £80.00 (including VAT) paid for in cash
23 Nov	Paid salaries by BACS, £1,357.00 (no VAT)
23 Nov	Paid an invoice for £468.25 from Wyvern Cement Company (a creditor) by cheque for £458.25 and receiving £10.00 discount for prompt settlement
23 Nov	Bought stationery £85.25 + VAT, paying by cheque
23 Nov	Cash purchases of £340.40 (including VAT) paid for in cash

The rate of Value Added Tax is 17.5%

Account numbers are to be used as follows:

Main ledger account codes (extract):	
1000	Cash book
2500	Purchases ledger control
3500	Discount received
4500	Purchases
6000	VAT
7000	Salaries and wages
7500	Sundry

Subsidiary (purchases) ledger account codes (extract):	
120	Broughton Brick Company
150	Broad Timber Limited
890	Wyvern Cement

Using the layouts on the next three pages, you are to:

- Enter the above payments on page 45 of the analysed cash book of Martin Peters (VAT amounts should be rounded down to the nearest penny).
- Total the money columns at 23 November.
- Show the entries to be made in the main ledger and the subsidiary (purchases) ledger.

ACCOUNT NO 1000 CASH BOOK (PAYMENTS)

CBP 45

Date 2007	Details	Reference	Cash £	Bank £	Discount received £	VAT £	Cash purchases £	Subsidiary (purchases) ledger £	Salaries and wages £	Sundry £	Subsidiary (purchases) ledger code
Main ledger codes		DR									
		CR									

MAIN LEDGER

2500 Purchases Ledger Control

Date	Details	Folio	Amount	Date	Details	Folio	Amount
2007			£	2007			£

3500 Discount Received

Date	Details	Folio	Amount	Date	Details	Folio	Amount
2007			£	2007			£

4500 Purchases

Date	Details	Folio	Amount	Date	Details	Folio	Amount
2007			£	2007			£

6000 VAT

Date	Details	Folio	Amount	Date	Details	Folio	Amount
2007			£	2007			£

7000 Salaries and Wages

Date	Details	Folio	Amount	Date	Details	Folio	Amount
2007			£	2007			£

MAIN LEDGER

				7500 Sundry				
Date	Details	Folio	Amount	Date	Details	Folio	Amount
2007			£	2007			£

SUBSIDIARY (PURCHASES) LEDGER

				120 Broughton Brick Company				
Date	Details	Folio	Amount	Date	Details	Folio	Amount
2007			£	2007			£

				150 Broad Timber Limited				
Date	Details	Folio	Amount	Date	Details	Folio	Amount
2007			£	2007			£

				890 Wyvern Cement				
Date	Details	Folio	Amount	Date	Details	Folio	Amount
2007			£	2007			£

16 PETTY CASH BOOK

16.1 A company operates its petty cash book using the imprest system. The imprest amount is £250.00. At the end of a particular period the analysis columns are totalled to give the following amounts:

VAT £13.42; postages £29.18; travel £45.47; stationery £33.29; sundry £18.54

How much cash will be required to restore the imprest amount for the next period?

16.2 You work as an accounts assistant in the offices of Hi-Tech Trading Company, a VAT-registered business. One of your responsibilities is to maintain the petty cash records and you are authorised to approve petty cash vouchers up to a value of £20 each. How will you deal with the following discrepancies and queries?

- A petty cash voucher for stationery is submitted to you for £12.50; the till receipt from the stationery shop shows a total of £10.00.

- A petty cash voucher for travelling expenses is submitted to you for £25.50; a rail ticket for this value is attached.

- The total of the analysis columns of the petty cash book differs from the total payments column.

- A colleague asks about the imprest amount and where you keep the keys to the petty cash box.

16.3 The cashier where you work as an accounts assistant has asked you to balance the petty cash book for the week ending 16 May 2007. The petty cash book is kept on the imprest system and, at the end of each week, cash is withdrawn from the main cash book to restore the imprest amount to £100.00.

The petty cash book is as follows:

Receipts	Date	Details	Voucher No	Total Payment	Analysis columns				
					VAT	Postages	Travel	Meals	Stationery
£	2007			£	£	£	£	£	£
100.00	12 May	Balance b/d							
	12 May	Travel	461	6.50			6.50		
	13 May	Meal allowance	462	6.11				6.11	
	13 May	Stationery	463	8.46	1.26				7.20
	13 May	Taxi	464	5.17	0.77		4.40		
	14 May	Stationery	465	4.70	0.70				4.00
	14 May	Travel	466	3.50			3.50		
	14 May	Postages	467	4.50		4.50			
	15 May	Bus fares	468	3.80			3.80		
	15 May	Catering	469	10.81	1.61			9.20	
	16 May	Postages	470	3.50		3.50			
	16 May	Stationery	471	7.52	1.12				6.40
	16 May	Travel	472	6.45			6.45		

You are to:

- restore the imprest amount of petty cash to £100.00, making the appropriate entry (note: the main cash book entry for this transaction need not be shown)

- balance the petty cash book at 16 May 2007, bringing down the balance on 17 May

16.4 You work as an accounts assistant in the offices of Wyvern Printers plc, a company which specialises in printing colour supplements for newspapers. Your supervisor is the main cashier. One of your tasks includes responsibility for all aspects of petty cash.

The accounting procedures manual of Wyvern Printers includes the following references to petty cash:

- A petty cash book is to be maintained using the imprest system.

- The imprest amount at the beginning of each week is to be £250.

- The maximum amount which can be drawn from petty cash is £50 in any one transaction.

- The petty cashier can authorise petty cash vouchers up to £25 for any one transaction; amounts above £25 and up to £50 can be authorised by the main cashier.

- All petty cash transactions must be recorded on petty cash vouchers which are to be

  - numbered in sequence

  - accompanied by relevant supporting documentation

- Authorised petty cash vouchers are to be recorded in a petty cash book with analysis columns for Value Added Tax, Postages, Travel, Stationery, Sundries.

- At the end of each week

  - cash is to be drawn from the main cashier to restore the imprest amount

  - the petty cash book is to be balanced ready for the following week

  - a posting sheet is to be prepared and passed to the main cashier

In addition you know that petty cash claims include VAT at the current rate of 17.5%, except for postages, rail and bus travel, newspapers and magazines which are either zero-rated or exempt from VAT.

During the week commencing 15 January 2007 several petty cash vouchers, together with supporting documentation, are passed to you by members of staff. The petty cash vouchers are shown on the next two pages, and the supporting documentation on the two pages following (pages 87 and 88).

You are to:

- Refer to the petty cash vouchers and supporting documentation – on the next four pages – and, for each claim you are satisfied with, you are to sign in the 'authorised' section; the authorised vouchers are to be numbered in sequence beginning with the number 352.

- For any petty cash claims you are unable to process, you are to write a memorandum to the main cashier explaining the reasons.

- Write up the petty cash book for the week commencing 15 January 2007 starting with an imprest balance of £250, and recording the petty cash vouchers that you have authorised.

- Total the analysis columns and prepare a posting sheet which shows the entries to be recorded in the main ledger at the end of the week, on 19 January. Account numbers need not be shown.

- Restore the imprest amount of petty cash to £250.00 by transfer from the cash book.

- Balance the petty cash book at 19 January 2007 and bring down the balance on 22 January.

Vouchers for the week beginning 15 January 2007 (continued on the next page)

petty cash voucher	no. _____		
	date 18/01/2007		
description	**amount**		
		£	p
Postages		25	25
		25	25
signature M Gono			
authorised			

petty cash voucher	no. _____		
	date 18/01/2007		
description	**amount**		
		£	p
Stationery		14	10
		14	10
signature J Jones			
authorised			

petty cash voucher	no. _____		
	date 18/01/2007		
description	**amount**		
		£	p
Taxi fare		4	70
		4	70
signature J Jones			
authorised			

petty cash voucher	no. _____		
	date 18/01/2007		
description	**amount**		
		£	p
Meal allowance		6	11
		6	11
signature C Bellamy			
authorised			

petty cash voucher	no. _____		
	date 17/01/2007		
description	**amount**		
		£	p
Travel		22	85
		22	85
signature J Jones			
authorised			

petty cash voucher	no. _____		
	date 17/01/2007		
description	**amount**		
		£	p
Postages		17	00
		17	00
signature M Gonzalez			
authorised			

petty cash voucher		no. _____
		date _16/01/2007_
description	**amount**	
	£	p
Travel	13	50
	13	50
signature M Foster		
authorised		

petty cash voucher		no. _____
		date _16/01/2007_
description	**amount**	
	£	p
Taxi	5	17
	5	17
signature J Carragher		
authorised		

petty cash voucher		no. _____
		date _16/01/2007_
description	**amount**	
	£	p
Stationery	4	70
	4	70
signature J Jones		
authorised		

petty cash voucher		no. _____
		date _15/01/2007_
description	**amount**	
	£	p
Stationery	8	46
	8	46
signature C Bellamy		
authorised		

petty cash voucher		no. _____
		date _15/01/2007_
description	**amount**	
	£	p
Meal allowance	6	11
	6	11
signature P Manesar		
authorised		

petty cash voucher		no. _____
		date _15/01/2007_
description	**amount**	
	£	p
Travel	16	50
	16	50
signature M Delpiero		
authorised		

Western Trains plc

PO Box 731, Weston WS1 1QQ

RECEIPT FOR RAIL TICKETS

Amount £ *16.50*

Date *15 Jan 2007*

Issued by *H Vaz*

Western Trains – working towards excellence

Wyvern Printers plc

MEAL ALLOWANCE

Date *15/01/2007*

Name *J. JONES*

Amount £ *6.11*

Authorised by *L. Luz, Manager*

Department code *08*

Stationery Suppliers Limited
8 High Street, Wyvern WV1 2AP

VAT registration: 491 7681 20

15 01 2007

Goods	7.20
VAT	1.26
Total	8.46
Tendered	10.00
Change	1.54

Please call again!

Crown Taxis

20 Lime Street, Wyvern WV3 1DS

Telephone: 01901 436941

Date *16/01/2007*

Received with thanks £ *5.17*

VAT registration: 495 7681 21

Stationery Suppliers Limited
8 High Street, Wyvern WV1 2AP

VAT registration: 491 7681 20

16 01 2007

Goods	4.00
VAT	0.70
Total	4.70
Tendered	10.00
Change	5.30

Please call again!

Western Trains plc

PO Box 731, Weston WS1 1QQ

RECEIPT FOR RAIL TICKETS

Amount £ *13.50*

Date *16/01/2007*

Issued by *J. Clark*

Western Trains – working towards excellence

```
POST OFFICE LIMITED
WYVERN HIGH STREET POSTSHOP
VAT REG 647240004    BRANCH NO 0096

15 01 2007                        1027

Parcel post
Total to pay                      17.00
Cash tendered                     20.00
Change                             3.00
    DON'T FORGET VALENTINE'S DAY!
           14th FEBRUARY
```

```
Western Trains plc
PO Box 731, Weston WS1 1QQ

RECEIPT FOR RAIL TICKETS

Amount          £ 22.85

Date            17/01/2007

Issued by       H Vaz

Western Trains – working towards excellence
```

```
Wyvern Printers plc

MEAL ALLOWANCE

Date              18 Jan 2007

Name              R. SINGH

Amount            £ 6.11

Authorised by     A. Eden, Manager

Department code   12
```

```
Crown Taxis
20 Lime Street, Wyvern WV3 1DS
Telephone: 01901 436941

Date                    18 Jan 2007

Received with thanks  £ 4.70

        VAT registration: 495 7681 21
```

```
Stationery Suppliers Limited
8 High Street, Wyvern WV1 2AP
VAT registration: 491 7681 20

              18 01 2007

Goods          12.00
VAT             2.10
Total          14.10
Tendered       20.00
Change          6.90
Please call again!
```

```
POST OFFICE LIMITED
WYVERN HIGH STREET POSTSHOP
VAT REG 647240004    BRANCH NO 0096

18 01 2007                    1536

Stamps
Total to pay                 25.25
Cash tendered                30.00
Change                        4.75
   DON'T FORGET VALENTINE'S DAY!
          14th FEBRUARY
```

17 FURTHER ASPECTS OF DOUBLE-ENTRY ACCOUNTS

17.1 Tom Griffiths set up in business on 1 March 2007 and registered for Value Added Tax. During the first month he has kept a cash book but, unfortunately, has made some errors:

Debit	Cash Book: Receipts				CBR
Date	Details	Folio	Discount allowed	Cash	Bank
2007			£	£	£
4 Mar	Office equipment*				1,175
12 Mar	Drawings			125	

Credit	Cash Book: Payments				CBP
Date	Details	Folio	Discount received	Cash	Bank
2007			£	£	£
3 Mar	Capital				6,500
5 Mar	Bank loan				2,500
7 Mar	Wages				250
10 Mar	Commission received*			141	
12 Mar	Rent paid				200
17 Mar	Van*				7.050

The items with asterisks (*) include Value Added Tax

Tom Griffiths has not got around to the other double-entry accounts.

You are to rewrite the cash book of Tom Griffiths, putting right his errors, and to draw up the other accounts, making the appropriate entries.

Notes:

- Use the current rate of Value Added Tax (17.5 % at the time of writing)

- Account numbers need not be used

- Separate books of prime entry need not be shown

17.2 Enter the following transactions into the double-entry book-keeping accounts of Caroline Yates, who is registered for Value Added Tax. Include a cash book receipts and a cash book payments, both with columns for cash and bank.

2007	
3 Nov	Started in business with capital of £75,000 in the bank
4 Nov	Bought a photocopier for £2,400 + VAT, paying by cheque
7 Nov	Received a bank loan of £70,000
10 Nov	Bought office premises £130,000, paying by cheque
12 Nov	Paid rates of £3,000, by cheque
14 Nov	Bought office fittings £1,520 + VAT, paying by cheque
17 Nov	Received commission of £400 + VAT, in cash
18 Nov	Drawings in cash £125
20 Nov	Paid wages £250, by cheque
25 Nov	Returned some of the office fittings (unsuitable) and received a refund cheque for £200 + VAT
28 Nov	Received commission £200 + VAT, by cheque

Notes:

- Use the current rate of Value Added Tax (17.5% at the time of writing)

- Account numbers need not be used

- Separate books of prime entry need not be shown

17.3 A friend of yours, Natasha Williams, runs a catering business which supplies food and drink to companies for special events. You keep the 'books' of the business which is registered for VAT.

Natasha tells you about a customer, Mereford Marketing, for whom she provided tea and coffee for their stand at the 'Two Counties Spring Show'. Despite sending monthly statements of account and 'chaser' letters she has still not been paid, and has recently heard that they have gone out of business. It is now 18 December 2007 and Natasha doesn't think she will be able to collect the amount due and asks you to write off the account as a bad debt.

You look up the account in the subsidiary (sales) ledger:

Dr			Mereford Marketing		Cr
2007		£	2007		£
25 Apr	Sales	141			

Natasha reminds you that, as VAT was charged on the original invoice, VAT can be reclaimed when writing off that debt.

You are to show:

- the journal entry made on 18 December 2007

- the transactions on Mereford Marketing's account in the subsidiary (sales) ledger

- bad debts written off account in the main ledger

- VAT account in the main ledger

- sales ledger control account in the main ledger

Note: account numbers need not be used

17.4 You are an accounts assistant at Osborne Electronics. A work experience student from the local college is with you today. The owner of the business authorises you to show the student the following non-routine transactions which are going through the accounts today, 16 November 2007:

- office equipment has been bought for £1,200 + VAT and paid for by cheque

- the owner of the business has paid in additional capital, £2,500 by cheque (no VAT)

- the account of a debtor, Tintern Travel, with a balance of £188 is to be written off as a bad debt (VAT-relief is available)

- a loan of £1,000 (no VAT) has been received from David Nazir by cheque

You are to:

(a) Explain to the student what each transaction represents and the double-entry book-keeping involved.

(b) Prepare a posting sheet for the transactions (account numbers need not be used).

17.5 Classify the following costs as either *capital expenditure* or *revenue expenditure*.

	capital expenditure	revenue expenditure
(a) building an extension to the factory		
(b) repairs to the existing factory		
(c) fuel for vehicles		
(d) purchase cost of vehicles		
(e) delivery cost of vehicles		
(f) cost of own materials used to repair the office		
(g) wages of own employees used to carry out repairs to the office		
(h) office salaries		

18 BALANCING THE CASH BOOK AND BANK RECONCILIATION

18.1 A firm's bank statement shows an overdraft of £600. Unpresented cheques total £250; outstanding lodgements total £1,000. What is the balance shown by the firm's cash book?

(a) £150

(b) £650

(c) £250 overdraft

(d) £150 overdraft

Answer (a) or (b) or (c) or (d)

18.2 Upon receipt of a bank statement, which one of the following must be written into the firm's cash book?

(a) cheque debited in error by the bank

(b) unpresented cheques

(c) BACS receipts

(d) outstanding lodgements

Answer (a) or (b) or (c) or (d)

18.3 Heath Traders Limited requires the bank statement and cash book balances (bank columns) to be reconciled. You are given the following information as at 30 June 2007:

- the bank columns of the cash book show an overdraft of £1,250 at the bank

- cheques for £140, £110 and £60 have been sent out in payment to various suppliers but have not yet been paid into the bank by those suppliers; they are recorded in the cash book

- a direct debit payment of £40 has been recorded by the bank, but has not yet been entered in the cash book

- a cheque for £600 has been recorded as a receipt in the cash book, and paid into the bank; it has not yet been credited by the bank

- bank charges amounting to £25 appear on the bank statement, but have not yet been entered in the cash book

- a BACS receipt from a customer for £250 appears on the bank statement, but has not yet been entered in the cash book

- the bank statement shows a closing bank overdraft of £1,355

You are to:

(a) write the cash book up-to-date at 30 June 2007

(b) prepare a bank reconciliation statement at 30 June 2007 which agrees the bank statement balance with the cash book balance

18.4 The bank columns of David Smith's cash book for March 2007 are as follows:

2007	Receipts	£	2007	Payments		£
1 Mar	Balance b/d	755.50	4 Mar	Curtis Ltd	001531	200.00
8 Mar	Johnson Limited	530.90	12 Mar	T Daniels	001532	327.40
29 Mar	Reid & Co	386.45	15 Mar	Smith & Co	001533	289.60
			16 Mar	Arnold & Sons	001534	327.20
			22 Mar	P Singh	001535	154.30

He received his bank statement which showed the following transactions for March 2007:

BANK STATEMENT				
Date	Details	Payments	Receipts	Balance
2007		£	£	£
1 Mar	Balance brought forward			855.50 CR
5 Mar	Cheque no 001530	100.00		755.50 CR
8 Mar	Cheque no 001531	200.00		555.50 CR
8 Mar	Credit		530.90	1,086.40 CR
15 Mar	BACS receipt: A J Trading		396.20	1,482.60 CR
22 Mar	Cheque no 001532	327.40		1,155.20 CR
24 Mar	Direct debit: Arley Finance	184.65		970.55 CR
25 Mar	Cheque no 001533	289.60		680.95 CR

You are to:

(a) write the cash book up-to-date at 31 March 2007, and show the balance carried down

(b) prepare a bank reconciliation statement at 31 March 2007 which agrees the bank statement balance with the cash book balance

18.5 You are the trainee cashier at Durning Traders Limited, working under the supervision of the office manager. The bank columns of the company's cash book for the week commencing 7 June 2007 are as follows:

2007	Receipts	£	2007	Payments		£
7 Jun	Balance b/d	986.40	7 Jun	Mega Books Ltd	654321	406.29
7 Jun	Wyvern Council	428.15	7 Jun	Cash	654322	250.00
10 Jun	Abacus & Co	752.00	8 Jun	Western Telecom	654323	186.45
10 Jun	ITI Plc	552.16	10 Jun	Wages	654324	522.15
			11 Jun	College Supplies Ltd	654325	342.87

The bank statement was received which showed the following transactions for the week:

BANK STATEMENT				
Date	Details	Payments	Receipts	Balance
2007		£	£	£
7 Jun	Balance brought forward			1,186.40 CR
7 Jun	Cheque no 654320	200.00		986.40 CR
7 Jun	Credit		428.15	1,414.55 CR
7 Jun	Cheque no 654322	250.00		1,164.55 CR
10 Jun	DD: Westmid Finance Co	107.25		1,057.30 CR
10 Jun	Cheque no 654324	522.15		535.15 CR
10 Jun	Credit		752.00	1,287.15 CR
10 Jun	BACS: Johnson Plc		398.52	1,685.67 CR
11 Jun	Cheque no 654321	406.29		1,279.38 CR
11 Jun	Cheque no 888901	50.00		1,229.38 CR
11 Jun	Bank charges	17.50		1,211.88 CR
SO Standing Order **DD** Direct Debit **BACS** Automated Transfer				

You are to:

(a) write the cash book up-to-date for the week commencing 7 June 2007, and show the balance carried down

(b) prepare a bank reconciliation statement at 11 June 2007 which agrees the bank statement balance with the cash book balance

(c) write a memorandum to the office manager regarding any matter that you think should be queried with the bank (use the blank memorandum printed on the next page)

MEMORANDUM

To

From

Date

18.6   You work as an accounts assistant in the office of Speciality Paints Limited, a company which buys special types of paints and other finishes from the manufacturers and sells them in your area to local businesses. This week the cashier, who is responsible for keeping the company's cash book is away on holiday. You have been asked to carry out her work for the week commencing 8 September 2007.

At the start of the week the cash book has a balance at bank of £802.50, and cash in hand of £120.68. The following are the transactions to be entered in the cash book for the week:

Cheques received from debtors

8 Sep	£389.51 from Wyvern County Council, in full settlement of an invoice for £398.01
10 Sep	£451.20 from J Jones & Company
12 Sep	£458.25 from Building Supplies Limited, in full settlement of an invoice for £468.25

Note: all cheques received are banked on the day of receipt.

Cheques drawn

8 Sep	Cheque no 123451 for £263.49, payee ITI Paint Division Limited, a creditor, in full settlement of an invoice for £269.24
9 Sep	Cheque no 123452 for £100.00, payee Wyvern Charities
9 Sep	Cheque no 123453 for £169.75, payee United Telecom plc
10 Sep	Cheque no 123454 for £394.20, payee Wages
11 Sep	Cheque no 123455 for £160.38, payee Paint Manufacturing plc, in full settlement of an invoice for £163.88

Cash received from debtors

9 Sep	£27.50 from T Lewis
12 Sep	£22.91 from H Simms, in full settlement of an invoice for £23.41

Cash paid

11 Sep	£88.50 for casual labour

At the end of the week, the bank statement, shown on the next page, is received.

You are to:

- enter the transactions for the week in the three-column (with columns for discount, cash, bank) cash book of Speciality Paints Limited

- check the bank statement and write the cash book (bank columns) up-to-date with any items appearing on the bank statement that need to be recorded in the cash book

- balance the cash book at 12 September 2007, and show the discount accounts as they will appear in the firm's main ledger

- prepare a bank reconciliation statement which agrees the bank statement balance with the cash book balance

- write a memorandum to the office manager regarding any matter that you consider should be queried with the bank (use the blank memorandum printed on page 90)

National Bank PLC

Branch Mereford

Account Speciality Paints Ltd

Account number 12345678   **Statement number** 45   **Date** 12 Sep 2007

Date	Details	Payments	Receipts	Balance
2007		£	£	£
8 Sep	Balance brought forward			802.50 Cr
8 Sep	Credit		389.51	1,192.01 Cr
9 Sep	Cheque 123452	100.00		1,092.01 Cr
9 Sep	DD Wyvern Hire Purchase	85.50		1,006.51 Cr
10 Sep	Cheque 123454	394.20		612.31 Cr
10 Sep	Credit		451.20	1,063.51 Cr
10 Sep	BACS Johnson & Co		125.50	1,189.01 Cr
11 Sep	Cheque 123451	263.49		925.52 Cr
11 Sep	Cheque 874111	25.00		900.52 Cr
12 Sep	Bank charges	12.50		888.02 Cr

SO Standing Order   **DD** Direct Debit   **BACS** Automated Transfer

MEMORANDUM

To

From

Date

19 USING THE JOURNAL AND RECONCILING CONTROL ACCOUNTS

19.1 Which one of the following transactions will be recorded in the journal?

(a) credit purchase of goods

(b) credit purchase of a fixed asset

(c) goods returned by a debtor

(d) cash sale of goods

Answer (a) or (b) or (c) or (d)

19.2 Which one of the following transactions will not be recorded in the journal?

(a) opening entries of a new business

(b) goods taken by the owner for her own use

(c) petty cash payment for office window cleaning

(d) writing off a bad debt

Answer (a) or (b) or (c) or (d)

19.3 Mohammed Pazir started in business on 1 February 2007 with the following assets and liabilities:

	£
Vehicle	6,500
Fixtures and fittings	2,800
Stock	4,100
Cash	150
Loan from uncle	5,000

You are to prepare Mohammed's opening journal entry showing clearly his capital at 1 February 2007.

19.4 Your friend, Sam Huntley, has recently set up in business selling electrical fittings and parts to both trade customers and members of the public. Her business is not yet registered for VAT.

You are helping Sam with the book-keeping. She has given you the list of business transactions shown on page 93 and asks for your help in identifying for each transaction:

• the book of prime entry

• the account to be debited

• the account to be credited

Her book-keeping system comprises a main ledger, with a subsidiary (sales) ledger and a subsidiary (purchases) ledger.

You are to complete the table on the next page with the information that Sam requires.

19.5 You work as an accounts assistant for James & Sons Limited. The company buys office furniture and stationery in bulk from the manufacturers and then sells smaller quantities on credit to local businesses.

Today the accounts supervisor has asked you to reconcile the sales ledger control account with the total of the subsidiary (sales) ledger. The information which follows is available to you.

Summary of transactions with credit customers in July 2007:

	£
Balance of debtors at 1 July 2007	64,626
Credit sales	72,310
Money received from credit customers	80,055
Discount allowed	90
Sales returns from credit customers	1,462
Bad debt written off	125

The following balances were shown in the subsidiary (sales) ledger at 31 July 2007:

	£	
A-Z Supplies Limited	8,394	debit
Doyle & Company	10,635	debit
Edgington and Sons	6,125	debit
Kernow Model Company	3,276	debit
Mereford Garden Centre	9,112	debit
Pembridge plc	13,236	debit
Wyvern Traders	4,516	debit

You are to:

(a) Prepare a sales ledger control account for July 2007 from the details above. The account is to be balanced at 31 July 2007 to show the balance carried down to next month.

(b) Reconcile the sales ledger control account with the total of the subsidiary ledger in the following format:

	£
Sales ledger control account balance as at 31 July 2007	
Total of subsidiary (sales) ledger accounts as at 31 July 2007	
Difference	

(c) If there is a difference calculated in (b) above, what do you think might have caused it?

19.4 See Activity on page 91

Business transaction		Book of prime entry	Account to be debited	Account to be credited
(a)	sold goods on credit to Aztec Electrics			
(b)	goods purchased on credit from United Supplies plc			
(c)	Aztec Electrics returns faulty goods – a credit note is issued			
(d)	bought office equipment on credit from Beacon Office Limited			
(e)	sold goods for cash			
(f)	Sam withdraws cash from the bank as drawings			
(g)	wrote off an account in the subsidiary (sales) ledger as a bad debt			
(h)	paid a creditor by cheque			

19.6 You work as an accounts assistant for Beacon Surf Limited. The company runs a large surf supplies shop overlooking a popular beach in Cornwall.

Today the accounts supervisor has asked you to reconcile the purchases ledger control account with the total of the subsidiary (purchases) ledger. The information which follows is available to you.

Summary of transactions with credit suppliers in May 2007:

	£
Balance of creditors at 1 May 2007	42,106
Goods purchased on credit	31,473
Paid creditors	25,236
Discount received	220
Goods returned to suppliers	2,048

The following balances were shown in the subsidiary (purchases) ledger at 31 May 2007:

	£	
Boards 'R Us	12,056	credit
Durning & Company	110	debit
Fistral Surf	4,872	credit
New Wave Limited	8,169	credit
Performance Clothing Limited	15,238	credit
Surf Supplies Limited	3,294	credit
Zelah Traders	2,996	credit

You are to:

(a) Prepare a purchases ledger control account for May 2007 from the details above. The account is to be balanced at 31 May 2007 to show the balance carried down to next month.

(b) Reconcile the purchases ledger control account with the total of the subsidiary ledger in the following format:

	£
Purchases ledger control account balance as at 31 May 2007	
Total of subsidiary (purchases) ledger accounts as at 31 May 2007	_____
Difference	_____

(c) If there is a difference calculated in (b) above, what do you think might have caused it?

19.7 Bissoe Limited keeps a petty cash control account in the main ledger and the petty cash book is the subsidiary account. Petty cash book is kept on the imprest method, and the imprest amount is £200.

The following petty cash transactions took place in June 2007:

1 Jun   Balance of petty cash book brought down, £200

30 Jun   Total of payments made from petty cash during the month, £111

30 Jun   Imprest amount restored by transfer from the bank

You are to:

(a) Enter the transactions for June 2007 into the firm's petty cash control account, showing clearly the balance carried down.

(b) State *one* other check you would carry out to ensure that the petty cash book is correct.

20 INITIAL TRIAL BALANCE AND CORRECTION OF ERRORS

20.1 The following are the business transactions of Robert Jefferson, a bookshop owner, for the months of January and February 2007:

Transactions for January

2007

1 Jan	Started in business with capital of £5,000 in the bank
2 Jan	Paid rent on premises £200, by cheque
3 Jan	Bought shop fittings £2,000, by cheque
6 Jan	Bought stock of books £2,500, on credit from Northam Publishers
8 Jan	Book sales £1,200, paid into bank
9 Jan	Book sales £1,000, paid into bank
13 Jan	Bought books £5,000, on credit from Broadheath Books
15 Jan	Book sales £1,500 to Teme School, a cheque being received
17 Jan	Book sales, £1,250, paid into bank
20 Jan	Bought books from Financial Publications £2,500, by cheque
23 Jan	Teme School returned unsuitable books £580, cheque refund sent
30 Jan	Sold books on credit to Wyvern College, £1,095

Transactions for February

2007

3 Feb	Book sales £2,510, paid into bank
5 Feb	Paid rent on premises £200, by cheque
7 Feb	Bought shop fittings £1,385, by cheque
10 Feb	Book sales £3,875, paid into bank
11 Feb	Sent cheque, £2,500, to Northam Publishers
13 Feb	Bought books £1,290, on credit from Northam Publishers
14 Feb	Sent cheque, £5,000, to Broadheath Books
17 Feb	Book sales £1,745, paid into bank
18 Feb	Wyvern College returned books, £250
21 Feb	Book sales £1,435, paid into bank
24 Feb	Bought books £1,250, on credit from Associated Publishers
28 Feb	Book sales £3,900, paid into bank

You are to:

(a)   Record the January transactions in his double-entry accounts. Balance all the accounts that have more than one transaction at 31 January 2007

(b)   Draw up a trial balance at 31 January 2007

(c)   Record the February transactions in his double-entry accounts. Balance all the accounts that have more than one transaction at 28 February 2007

(d)   Draw up a trial balance at 28 February 2007

Notes:

*   *Robert Jefferson's book-keeping system comprises a cash book (which has a money column for bank only), a main ledger (which includes purchases ledger and sales ledger control accounts), and subsidiary purchases and sales ledgers*

*   *day books are not required*

*   *Robert Jefferson is not registered for VAT*

20.2   The book-keeper of Lorna Fox has extracted the following list of balances as at 31 March 2007:

	£
Purchases	96,250
Sales	146,390
Sales returns	8,500
Administration expenses	10,240
Wages	28,980
Telephone	3,020
Interest paid	2,350
Travel expenses	1,045
Premises	125,000
Machinery	30,000
Stock at 1 January 2007	8,240
Debtors	12,150
Bank overdraft	1,050
Cash	150
Creditors	9,619
Value Added Tax (credit balance)	2,876
Loan from bank	20,000
Drawings	9,450
Capital	155,440

You are to:

(a)   Produce the trial balance at 31 March 2007.

(b)   Take any three debit balances and any three credit balances and explain to a trainee who has just started work with the accounts department why they are listed as such, and what this means to the business.

20.3   The purchase of £20 of stationery has been debited to office equipment account. This is:

(a)   an error of original entry

(b)   an error of principle

(c)   a mispost/error of commission

(d)   a reversal of entries

Answer (a) or (b) or (c) or (d)

20.4   A credit purchase of £63 from T Billington has been entered in the accounts as £36. This is:

(a)   a reversal of entries

(b)   an error of original entry

(c)   a compensating error

(d)   an error of omission

Answer (a) or (b) or (c) or (d)

20.5   Telephone expenses of £250 paid by cheque have been debited to the bank columns of the cash book and credited to the telephone expenses account. Which of the following entries will correct the error?

	Debit		*Credit*	
(a)	Bank	£250	Telephone expenses	£250
(b)	Telephone expenses	£250	Bank	£250
(c)	Bank	£250	Telephone expenses	£250
	Bank	£250	Telephone expenses	£250
(d)	Telephone expenses	£250	Bank	£250
	Telephone expenses	£250	Bank	£250

Answer (a) or (b) or (c) or (d)

20.6 Fill in the missing words from the following sentences:

(a) "You made an error of .... when you debited the cost of diesel fuel for the van to Vans Account."

(b) "I've had the book-keeper from D Jones Limited on the 'phone concerning the statements of account that we sent out the other day. She says that there is a sales invoice charged that she knows nothing about. I wonder if we have done a .... and it should be for T Jones' account?"

(c) "There is a 'bad figure' on a purchases invoice – we have read it as £35 when it should be £55. It has gone through our accounts wrongly so we have an error of .... to put right."

(d) "Although the trial balance balanced last week, I've since found an error of £100 in the calculation of the balance of sales account. We will need to check the other balances as I think we may have a .... error."

(e) "Who was in charge of that trainee last week? He has entered the payment for the electricity bill on the debit side of the bank and on the credit side of electricity – a .... of ...."

(f) "I found this purchase invoice from last week in amongst the copy letters. As we haven't put it through the accounts we have an error of ...."

20.7 A friend, who is just beginning her studies of book-keeping comments:

- "if the trial balance totals agree it is proof that the book-keeping entries are 100 per cent correct"

- "I wouldn't know where to start looking if the trial balance totals did not agree."

What would you reply to your friend?

20.8 The following list of balances was taken from the accounting records of Len Lewis on 31 August 2007:

	£
Office equipment	18,750
Stock	4,525
Debtors	10,294
Creditors	8,731
Bank overdraft	879
Cash	354
VAT (credit balance)	1,396
Capital	25,000
Drawings	15,391
Sales	175,686
Purchases	97,243
Sales returns	3,604
Purchases returns	2,856
General expenses	64,387

On 3 September 2007 the following errors and omissions were discovered:

- a sales invoice for £400 + VAT had not been entered in the sales day book
- a cheque for £625 from a debtor had not been recorded in the accounts
- Len Lewis had taken drawings of £300 by cheque but no entries had been made in the accounts
- a purchases invoice for £200 + VAT had been entered twice in the purchases day book

You are to: prepare a trial balance for Len Lewis' business at 31 August 2007 after adjusting for the above errors and omissions.

20.9 You have recently taken over writing up the double-entry accounts of B Brick (Builders). You have found a number of errors made by the previous book-keeper as follows:

(a) Credit purchase of goods for £85 from J Stone has not been entered in the accounts

(b) A cheque for £155 received from Roger Williams, a debtor, has been credited to the account of another debtor, William Rogers

(c) Diesel fuel costing £30 has been debited to vehicles account

(d) A credit sale for £154 to T Potter has been entered in the accounts as £145

(e) Both purchases returns account and wages account have been overcast by £100

You are to take each error in turn and:

- state the type of error
- show the correcting journal entry

Notes:

- *the accounting system comprises a main ledger (which includes purchases ledger and sales ledger control accounts), and subsidiary purchases and sales ledgers*
- *VAT is to be ignored*
- *use today's date for the journal entries*

20.10 Tracey Truslove is the book-keeper for Mereford Traders Limited. At 30 June 2007 she is unable to balance the trial balance. The difference, £149 credit, is placed to a suspense account pending further investigation.

The following errors are later found:

(a) Purchases account is undercast by £100.

(b) A cheque for £95 for the purchase of stationery has been recorded in the stationery account as £59.

(c) Rent received of £205 has been debited to both the rent received account and the bank account.

(d) Vehicles expenses of £125 have not been entered in the expenses account.

You are to:

- make journal entries to correct the errors
- show the suspense account after the errors have been corrected

Note: VAT is to be ignored; the corrections are to be made on 9 July 2007.

21 USING THE TRIAL BALANCE

The following background information is common to both Student Activities:

You work as an accounts assistant for 'Hotspot Barbecues'. The company manufactures barbecues and accessories, and sells them to garden centres, country shops, and direct to the public. Hotspot Barbecues is registered for VAT.

Your job in the accounts department is principally concerned with the subsidiary purchases and sales ledgers and also with aspects of the main ledger. Main ledger contains purchases ledger and sales ledger control accounts, which form part of the double-entry. Individual accounts of creditors and debtors are kept in subsidiary ledgers.

21.1 Today is 1 August 2007 and you are working on the subsidiary (purchases) ledger and main ledger sections of the accounting system.

Transactions

The following transactions all took place on 1 August 2007 and have been entered into the relevant books of prime entry as shown below. No entries have yet been made into the ledger system. The VAT rate is 17.5%.

PURCHASES DAY BOOK

Date 2007	Details	Invoice No	Total £	VAT £	Net £
1 Aug	Reade Manufacturing	794	1,175	175	1,000
1 Aug	Reed Supplies Ltd	201	1,645	245	1,400
1 Aug	Bourne Limited	387	1,880	280	1,600
1 Aug	Eveshore Services	924	2,350	350	2,000
	TOTALS		7,050	1,050	6,000

PURCHASES RETURNS DAY BOOK

Date 2007	Details	Credit Note No	Total £	VAT £	Net £
1 Aug	Eveshore Services	CN 68	235	35	200
1 Aug	Reed Supplies Ltd	CN 32	517	77	440
	TOTALS		752	112	640

CASH BOOK

Date 2007	Details	Discount Allowed	Bank £	Date 2007	Details	Discount Received	Bank £
1 Aug	Balance b/d		4,200	1 Aug	Bourne Limited		2,500
1 Aug	Rent received		500	1 Aug	Reade Manufacturing	75	2,925
1 Aug	Balance c/d		770	1 Aug	Bank charges		45
			5,470			75	5,470

Balances to be inserted in ledger accounts

The following balances are relevant to you at the start of the day on 1 August 2007:

	£
Credit suppliers:	
Bourne Limited	3,840
Eveshore Services	2,330
Reade Manufacturing	3,000
Reed Supplies Limited	3,690
Purchases ledger control	12,860
Purchases	197,384
Purchases returns	2,590
Discount received	710
Rent received	3,250
Bank charges	335
VAT (credit balance)	3,980

Balances to be transferred to trial balance

	£
Premises	125,000
Machinery	30,000
Vehicles	28,200
Stock	15,590
Cash	200
Sales ledger control	35,390
Capital	120,000
Sales	376,332
Sales returns	3,640
Discount allowed	845
Wages and salaries	68,140
Electricity	5,260
Bad debts written off	434
Vehicle expenses	3,174
Rates paid	1,930

Task 1.1   Enter the opening balances listed on the previous page into the following accounts given on the next four pages:

Subsidiary (purchases) ledger

Bourne Limited
Eveshore Services
Reade Manufacturing
Reed Supplies Limited

Main ledger
Purchases ledger control
Purchases
Purchases returns
Discount received
Rent received
Bank charges
VAT

Task 1.2   From the day books and cash book shown on pages 102 and 103 make the relevant entries in the accounts in the subsidiary (purchases) ledger and the main ledger.

Task 1.3   Balance the accounts showing clearly the balances carried down at 1 August 2007 (closing balance).

Task 1.4 Now that you have closed the above accounts, show clearly the balance brought down at 2 August 2007 (opening balance). Demonstrate a reconciliation of the balance of purchases ledger control account with the subsidiary accounts.

Task 1.5 Transfer the balances calculated in task 1.3, and from the cash book, to the trial balance shown on page 108.

Task 1.6 Transfer the remaining balances shown at the top of page 104 to the trial balance and total each column. The debit column and credit column totals should be the same.

Tasks 1.1, 1.2, 1.3 and 1.4

SUBSIDIARY (PURCHASES) LEDGER

Bourne Limited

Date	Details	Amount £	Date	Details	Amount £

Eveshore Services

Date	Details	Amount £	Date	Details	Amount £

Reade Manufacturing

Date	Details	Amount £	Date	Details	Amount £

SUBSIDIARY (PURCHASES) LEDGER

Reed Supplies Limited

Date	Details	Amount £	Date	Details	Amount £

Reconciliation of purchases ledger control account

	1 Aug 2007 £	2 Aug 2007 £
Bourne Limited		
Eveshore Services		
Reade Manufacturing		
Reed Supplies Limited		
Purchases ledger control account (see below)		

MAIN LEDGER

Purchases ledger control

Date	Details	Amount £	Date	Details	Amount £

Purchases

Date	Details	Amount £	Date	Details	Amount £

MAIN LEDGER

Purchases returns

Date	Details	Amount £	Date	Details	Amount £

Discount received

Date	Details	Amount £	Date	Details	Amount £

Rent received

Date	Details	Amount £	Date	Details	Amount £

Bank charges

Date	Details	Amount £	Date	Details	Amount £

MAIN LEDGER

VAT

Date	Details	Amount £	Date	Details	Amount £

Tasks 1.5 and 1.6

TRIAL BALANCE AS AT 1 AUGUST 2007

	Debit £	Credit £
Premises	....	....
Machinery	....	....
Vehicles	....	....
Stock	....	....
Bank	....	....
Cash	....	....
Sales ledger control	....	....
Capital	....	....
Sales	....	....
Sales returns	....	....
Discount allowed	....	....
Wages and salaries	....	....
Electricity	....	....
Bad debts written off	....	....
Vehicle expenses	....	....
Rates paid	....	....
Purchases ledger control	....	....
Purchases	....	....
Purchases returns	....	....
Discount received	....	....
Rent received	....	....
Bank charges	....	....
VAT	....	....
TOTAL	....	....

21.2 Today is 2 August 2007 and you are working on the main ledger and subsidiary (sales) ledger sections of the accounting system.

Transactions

The following transactions all took place on 2 August 2007 and have been entered into the relevant books of prime entry as shown below. No entries have yet been made into the ledger system. The VAT rate is 17.5%.

SALES DAY BOOK

Date 2007	Details	Invoice No	Total £	VAT £	Net £
2 Aug	Charlton Home Furnishings	504	940	140	800
2 Aug	Tauntone Country Store	505	1,175	175	1,000
2 Aug	A-Z Garden Centre	506	1,410	210	1,200
2 Aug	Charlton Home Furnishings	507	470	70	400
	TOTALS		3,995	595	3,400

SALES RETURNS DAY BOOK

Date 2007	Details	Credit Note No	Total £	VAT £	Net £
2 Aug	A-Z Garden Centre	CN 63	188	28	160
2 Aug	Tauntone Country Store	CN 64	329	49	280
	TOTALS		517	77	440

CASH BOOK

Date 2007	Details	Discount Allowed	Bank £	Date 2007	Details	Discount Received	Bank £
2 Aug	Charlton Home Furnishings	60	2,340	2 Aug	Balance b/d		770
				2 Aug	Wages and salaries		3,227
2 Aug	A-Z Garden Centre		1,000				
2 Aug	Balance c/d		657				
		60	3,997				3,997

Balances to be inserted in ledger accounts

The following balances are relevant to you at the start of the day on 2 August 2007:

£

Credit customers:

A-Z Garden Centre	2,052
Charlton Home Furnishings	12,400
Ralph's Gardens	141
Tauntone Country Store	20,797
Sales ledger control	35,390
Sales	376,332
Sales returns	3,640
Discount allowed	845
Vehicles	28,200
Vehicle expenses	3,174
Wages and salaries	68,140
VAT (credit balance)	3,042
Bad debts written off	434

Journal entries

The accounts supervisor asks you to make entries in the journal and the double-entry accounts for the following:

* the subsidiary (sales) ledger account balance in the name of Ralph's Gardens is to be written off as a bad debt; you are told that VAT relief is available on this debt

* an amount of £200 + VAT for vehicle expenses was debited to vehicles account in error on 26 July 2007

Balances to be transferred to trial balance

£

Premises	125,000
Machinery	30,000
Stock	15,590
Cash	200
Capital	120,000
Electricity	5,260
Rates paid	1,930
Purchases ledger control	13,658
Purchases	203,384
Purchases returns	3,230
Discount received	785
Rent received	3,750
Bank charges	380

Task 2.1   Enter the opening balances listed on the previous page into the following accounts given on the next four pages:

Subsidiary (sales) ledger

A-Z Garden Centre

Charlton Home Furnishings

Ralph's Gardens

Tauntone Country Store

Main ledger

Sales ledger control

Sales

Sales returns

Discount allowed

Vehicles

Vehicle expenses

Wages and salaries

VAT

Bad debts written off

Task 2.2   •   From the day books and cash book shown on page 109 make the relevant entries in the accounts in the subsidiary (sales) ledger and the main ledger.

•   Record the entries in the journal on page 115 (narratives are not required) for the transactions mentioned by the accounts supervisor and then enter the transactions into the relevant accounts.

Task 2.3   Balance the accounts showing clearly the balances carried down at 2 August 2007 (closing balance).

Task 2.4   Now that you have closed the above accounts, show clearly the balance brought down at 3 August 2007 (opening balance). Demonstrate a reconciliation of sales ledger control account with the subsidiary accounts.

Task 2.5   Transfer the balances calculated in task 2.3, and from the cash book, to the trial balance shown on page 116.

Task 2.6   Transfer the remaining balances shown at the bottom of page 110 to the trial balance and total each column. The debit column and credit column totals should be the same.

Tasks 2.1, 2.2, 2.3 and 2.4

SUBSIDIARY (SALES) LEDGER

A-Z Garden Centre

Date	Details	Amount £	Date	Details	Amount £

Charlton Home Furnishings

Date	Details	Amount £	Date	Details	Amount £

Ralph's Gardens

Date	Details	Amount £	Date	Details	Amount £

Tauntone Country Store

Date	Details	Amount £	Date	Details	Amount £

Reconciliation of sales ledger control account

	2 Aug 2007 £	3 Aug 2007 £
A-Z Garden Centre		
Charlton Home Furnishings		
Ralph's Gardens		
Tauntone Country Store		
Sales ledger control account (see below)		

MAIN LEDGER

Sales ledger control

Date	Details	Amount £	Date	Details	Amount £

Sales

Date	Details	Amount £	Date	Details	Amount £

Sales returns

Date	Details	Amount £	Date	Details	Amount £

MAIN LEDGER

Discount allowed

Date	Details	Amount £	Date	Details	Amount £

Vehicles

Date	Details	Amount £	Date	Details	Amount £

Vehicle expenses

Date	Details	Amount £	Date	Details	Amount £

Wages and salaries

Date	Details	Amount £	Date	Details	Amount £

MAIN LEDGER

VAT

Date	Details	Amount £	Date	Details	Amount £

Bad debts written off

Date	Details	Amount £	Date	Details	Amount £

JOURNAL

Date	Details	Debit	Credit

Tasks 2.5 and 2.6

TRIAL BALANCE AS AT 1 AUGUST 2007

	Debit £	Credit £
Premises	....	....
Machinery	....	....
Vehicles	....	....
Stock	....	....
Bank	....	....
Cash	....	....
Sales ledger control	....	....
Capital	....	....
Sales	....	....
Sales returns	....	....
Discount allowed	....	....
Wages and salaries	....	....
Electricity	....	....
Bad debts written off	....	....
Vehicle expenses	....	....
Rates paid	....	....
Purchases ledger control	....	....
Purchases	....	....
Purchases returns	....	....
Discount received	....	....
Rent received	....	....
Bank charges	....	....
VAT	....	....
TOTAL	....	....

**Practice Examination 1
The Garden Warehouse**

PRACTICE EXAMINATION 1
THE GARDEN WAREHOUSE

This exam paper is in TWO sections.

You must show competence in BOTH sections.

You should therefore attempt and aim to complete EVERY task in EACH section.

Section 1   Double entry bookkeeping and trial balance

Complete all 10 tasks

Section 2   Accounting processes

Complete all 20 tasks and questions

You should spend about 75 minutes on Section 1 and about 105 minutes on Section 2.

All essential calculations should be included within your answer, where appropriate.

Both sections are based on the business described below.

INTRODUCTION

- Marian Walker is the owner of The Garden Warehouse, a business which supplies gardening equipment.

- You are employed by the business as a bookkeeper.

- The business uses a manual accounting system.

- Double entry takes place in the Main (General) Ledger. Individual accounts of debtors and creditors are kept in subsidiary ledgers as memorandum accounts.

- Bank payments and receipts are recorded in the cash book, which is part of the double entry system.

- Assume today's date is 30 June 2005 unless you are told otherwise.

Section 1 – Double entry bookkeeping and trial balance

You should spend about 75 minutes on this section.

Note: Please show your answer by inserting a tick, text or figures, as appropriate.

Task 1.1

On 1 June there were opening balances on all the accounts in the Subsidiary (sales) ledger, which represent money owing to The Garden Warehouse.

Would the opening balances in the Subsidiary (sales) ledger be shown as debit or credit entries? Tick the correct answer

	✓
Debit	
Credit	

Task 1.2

On 1 June the following opening balances were in the Main ledger.

Would the opening balances in the Main ledger be shown as a debit or credit entry?

Account name	Amount £	Debit/Credit
Office equipment	3,500	
Sales	321,650	
Sales returns	15,800	
Sales ledger control	112,636	
Discount allowed	750	
Motor expenses	1,225	
Rent and rates	3,600	

Task 1.3

The following transactions all took place on 30 June 2005 and have been entered into the Sales day book as shown below. No entries have yet been made into the ledger system.

Sales day book

Date 2005	Details	Invoice Number	Total £	VAT at 17.5% £	Net £
30 June	Creations Ltd	849	2,115	315	1,800
30 June	Jackson and Company	850	9,870	1,470	8,400
30 June	Loxley Ltd	851	3,055	455	2,600
30 June	PTT Ltd	852	7,050	1,050	6,000
	Totals		22,090	3,290	18,800

(a)   What will be the entries in the Subsidiary (sales) ledger?

Account name	Amount £	Debit/Credit

(b)   What will be the entries in the Main ledger?

Account name	Amount £	Debit/Credit

Task 1.4

The following transactions all took place on 30 June 2005 and have been entered into the Sales returns day book as shown below. No entries have yet been made into the ledger system.

Sales returns day book

Date 2005	Details	Credit Note Number	Total £	VAT £	Net £
30 June	Creations Ltd	131	4,700	700	4,000
30 June	Loxley Ltd	132	423	63	360
	Totals		5,123	763	4,360

(a)   What will be the entries in the Subsidiary (sales) ledger?

Account name	Amount £	Debit/Credit

(b)   What will be the entries in the Main ledger?

Account name	Amount £	Debit/Credit

Task 1.5

The following transactions all took place on 30 June 2005 and have been entered into the Purchases day book as shown below. No entries have yet been made into the ledger system.

Purchases day book

Date 2005	Details	Invoice Number	Total £	VAT £	Net £
30 June	Lee Ltd	39872	3,525	525	3,000
30 June	Ball and McGee	128949	1,410	210	1,200
30 June	Horner and Company	Z694	12,690	1,890	10,800
30 June	H & H Ltd	H302	4,700	700	4,000
	Totals		22,325	3,325	19,000

(a)   What will be the entries in the Subsidiary (purchases) ledger?

Account name	Amount £	Debit/Credit

(b)   What will be the entries in the Main ledger?

Account name	Amount £	Debit/Credit

Task 1.6

The following transactions all took place on 30 June 2005 and have been entered into the Cash book as shown below. No entries have yet been made into the ledger system.

Cash book

Date	Receipt type	Details	Discount allowed £	Bank £	Date	Cheque details	Bank £
2005					2005		
30 June		Balance b/f		8,190	30 June	Motor expenses	350
30 June	BACS	Jackson and Company	100	3,650	30 June	Rent and rates	1,200
					30 June	Office equipment	3,250
					30 June	Croxford Ltd	2,000
					30 June	Balance c/d	5,040
			100	11,840			11,840
1 July		Balance b/d		5,040			

(a)   **What will be the entries to record this receipt and these payments in the Subsidiary (sales) ledger, Subsidiary (purchases) ledger and Main ledger?**

Subsidiary (sales) ledger

Account name	Amount £	Debit/Credit

Subsidiary (purchases) ledger

Account name	Amount £	Debit/Credit

Main ledger

Account name	Amount £	Debit/Credit

Task 1.7

The following two accounts are in the main ledger at the close of day on 30 June.

(a) Insert the balance carried down together with date and details.

(b) Insert the totals.

(c) Insert the balance brought down together with date and details.

Hotel expenses

Date 2005	Details	Amount £	Date 2005	Details	Amount £
1 June	Balance b/f	3,000			
26 June	Bank	595			
	Total			Total	

Loan from bank

Date 2005	Details	Amount £	Date 2005	Details	Amount £
18 June	Bank	700	1 June	Balance b/f	15,000
	Total			Total	

Task 1.8

Record the journal entries needed in the Main ledger to deal with the following.

Note: You do not need to give narratives. You may not need to use all the lines.

(a) An amount of £70 has been debited to the miscellaneous expenses account instead of the motor expenses account.

Account name	Amount £	Debit/Credit

(b) Purchases of £500 have been entered as £5,000 in the Main ledger account (ignore VAT).

Account name	Amount £	Debit/Credit

(c)   **A credit customer, L G Whitburn, has ceased trading. It owes The Garden Warehouse £200 plus VAT. The net amount and VAT must be written off in the Main ledger.**

Account name	Amount £	Debit/Credit

Task 1.9

During the month a trial balance was extracted which did not balance and an amount of £75 was credited to the suspense account. The following two errors have now been discovered.

(i)   Rent paid has been understated by £10.

(ii)   A figure in the heat and light account has been overstated by £85.

What entries are needed in the Main ledger to correct these errors?

Account name	Amount £	Debit/Credit

Task 1.10

Below is a list of balances to be transferred to the trial balance as at 30 June.

Place the figures in the debit or credit column, as appropriate, and total each column.

Account name	Amount £	Debit £	Credit £
Motor vehicles	5,200		
Office equipment	8,750		
Stock	17,000		
Cash at bank	5,040		
Petty cash control	60		
Sales ledger control	125,853		
Purchases ledger control	56,713		
VAT owing to HM Revenue & Customs	13,990		
Loan from bank	14,300		
Capital	32,373		
Sales	340,450		
Sales returns	20,160		
Purchases	206,511		
Purchases returns	862		
Discount received	248		
Discount allowed	850		
Wages	50,425		
Heat and light	963		
Motor expenses	1,645		
Rent and rates	4,810		
Travel expenses	1,650		
Hotel expenses	3,595		
Telephone	1,006		
Accountancy fees	2,530		
Bad debts written off	200		
Miscellaneous expenses	2,688		
Totals			

Section 2 – Accounting processes

You should spend about 105 minutes on this section.

Note 1: You do not need to adjust any accounts in Section 1 as part of any of the following tasks.

Note 2: Please show your answer by inserting a tick, text or figures, as appropriate.

Task 2.1

The Garden Warehouse has received the following purchase invoice.

Wentworth Supplies
18 High Street, Droitwich, Worcestershire, WR15 01W
Tel: 01943 567392

VAT Registration Number: 374 8219 00

To: The Garden Warehouse   29 June 2005
        2a Lower Parade
        Droitwich
        Worcestershire WR16 81S

INVOICE NO: P/1674

	£
	£
20 Garden spades	200.00
Less 10% trade discount	20.00
	180.00
VAT at 17.5%	30.87
Total	210.87

Terms: 2% settlement discount for payment within 7 days

Marian Walker has asked you to pay this invoice immediately.

(a)   **What is the amount to be paid to Wentworth Supplies?**

			✓
(i)	£206.65		
(ii)	£210.87		
(iii)	£207.27		
(iv)	£207.90		

(b)   **What is the purpose of a TRADE discount?**

		✓
(i)	To reward customers who pay in cash	
(ii)	To offer a lower price to an organisation within the same trade	
(iii)	To reduce the price of goods that are damaged	

(c)   **To which customers might The Garden Warehouse offer a BULK discount?**

		✓
(i)	Those placing large orders	
(ii)	Those with many branches	
(iii)	Those who have been customers for many years	

Task 2.2

If the VAT account in the Main ledger of The Garden Warehouse showed a debit balance, what would this indicate?

		✓
(i)	There had been an accounting error	
(ii)	The Garden Warehouse is entitled to a refund from HM Revenue & Customs	
(iii)	The Garden Warehouse does not have to charge VAT	

Task 2.3

On 1 June a manufacturer telephoned The Garden Warehouse and offered to supply some gardening equipment at a greatly reduced price. Marian Walker said she would think about it and reply by post. On 2 June Marian posted an acceptance of the offer to the supplier, who received it on 5 June.

What is the date on which the contract was formed?

			✓
(i)	1 June		
(ii)	2 June		
(iii)	5 June		

Task 2.4

The Garden Warehouse has just opened a credit account for a new supplier, Wright Brothers, which brings the total number of suppliers to 50.

(a)   Suggest an appropriate four-character alphanumeric ledger code for this account.

(b)   In which ledger would you expect to see this account?

		✓
(i)	Main ledger	
(ii)	Subsidiary (sales) ledger	
(iii)	Subsidiary (purchases) ledger	

Task 2.5

The following errors have been made in the accounting records of The Garden Warehouse. **Show whether the errors cause an imbalance in the trial balance.**

(a) **A purchase invoice is lost in the post and not received at The Garden Warehouse.**

			✓
(i)	The trial balance will balance		
(ii)	The trial balance will not balance		

(b) **Discount allowed has not been taken by a customer.**

			✓
(i)	The trial balance will balance		
(ii)	The trial balance will not balance		

(c) **A purchase invoice has been correctly entered in the Main ledger but omitted from the Subsidiary (purchases) ledger.**

			✓
(i)	The trial balance will balance		
(ii)	The trial balance will not balance		

(d) **An entry has been made to the Purchases and VAT accounts but omitted from the Purchases ledger control account.**

			✓
(i)	The trial balance will balance		
(ii)	The trial balance will not balance		

Task 2.6

A cheque has been received at The Garden Warehouse which has been dated 30 June 2004 and the bank will not accept it.

After what amount of time does a cheque become out of date?

	✓
3 months	
6 months	
12 months	
24 months	

Task 2.7

The Garden Warehouse buys goods from and sells goods to Pascoe Plants. It has been agreed to set off the amounts owing between them by a contra entry.

What accounts in the Main ledger of The Garden Warehouse would be adjusted to record this set-off?

Account name	Debit/Credit

Task 2.8

Which TWO items listed below would you expect to see in a Wages and salaries control account?

	✓
Total of net wages paid to employees	
Payment of Jackson Brothers for cleaning windows	
Total of trade union fee deductions	
Payment to creditors	

Task 2.9

The Garden Warehouse's transactions in June included the items listed below.

State whether each is a capital transaction or a revenue transaction.

Transaction	Capital or Revenue
Purchase of office stationery	
Annual decoration of offices	
Purchase of a delivery van	
Purchase of fuel for the delivery van	

Task 2.10

The petty cash control account shown below is in the Main ledger of The Garden Warehouse

Petty cash control

Date 2005	Details	Amount £	Date 2005	Details	Amount £
1 July	Balance b/f	60.00	5 July	Window cleaning	10.00
			10 July	Tea and coffee	5.00
			15 July	Stamps	30.00

What will be the amount required to restore the imprest level to £60?

£

Task 2.11

The Sale of Goods Act sets out what a customer is entitled to expect when buying goods from a shop.

Which one of the following statements is NOT included in this Act?

	✓
Goods must be of a satisfactory quality	
Goods must be worth the price asked	
Goods must be fit for purpose	
Goods must be as described	

Task 2.12

During the last VAT quarter sales amounted to £122,000 **plus VAT.** Purchases totalled £9,870 **including VAT.**

(a)   **What was the amount of VAT payable on sales made?**

(b)   **What was the amount of VAT included in the purchases figure?**

(c)   **What would have been the balance on the VAT account at the end of the quarter?**

(d)   **Is the amount you calculated in (c) above payable to HM Revenue & Customs or receivable from them?**

	✓
Payable to H M Revenue & Customs	
Receivable from H M Revenue & Customs	

Task 2.13

Marian Walker has given you a list of new customers and has asked you to apply credit limits to each account.

What is a credit limit?

	✓
The maximum amount allowed on any one invoice	
The term for a customer with no credit account	
The amount of time a debt may be outstanding	
The maximum amount allowed to be outstanding at any one time	

Task 2.14

The Garden Warehouse has received a cheque for £800 plus VAT for goods sold.

The customer does not have a credit account.

(a)   What will be the accounting entries required to record this receipt?

Account name	Amount £	Debit or Credit

(b)   Prepare the paying-in slip to pay this cheque into the bank on 1 July 2005, together with cash amounting to £120 and made up of two £20 notes, four £10 notes and eight £5 notes.

Date	Middle Bank plc Droitwich	£50 notes	
		£20 notes	
		£10 notes	
	Account The Garden Warehouse	£5 notes	
		£2 coin	
		£1 coin	
	Paid in by Marian Walker	Other coin	
No. of items		Total cash	
	49-20-40 39287594 78	Cheques, POs £	

Task 2.15

Which one of the following documents is used to accompany goods and, when provided in duplicate, acts as proof of delivery?

	✓
Sales order acknowledgement	
Advice note	
Delivery note	
Despatch note	

Task 2.16

What documents would The Garden Warehouse send out in each of the following circumstances?

		✓
(a) To accompany a cheque in payment of an account	Statement of account	
	Remittance advice	
	Credit note	
	Invoice	
	Confirmation order	
(b) To list unpaid invoices and ask for payment each month	Statement of account	
	Remittance advice	
	Credit note	
	Invoice	
	Confirmation order	
(c) To correct an overcharge on an invoice issued	Statement of account	
	Remittance advice	
	Credit note	
	Invoice	
	Confirmation order	

Task 2.17

(a) **This is a summary of transactions with suppliers during the month of June.**

Show whether each entry will be a debit or credit in the Purchases ledger control account.

		Debit/Credit
Balance of creditors at 1 June 2005	£53,386	
Goods bought on credit	£20,500	
Money paid to credit suppliers	£16,193	
Discounts received	£380	
Goods returned to credit suppliers	£600	

(b) **What will be the balance brought down on 1 July on the above account?**

		✓
Dr	£89,099	
Cr	£89,099	
Dr	£56,713	
Cr	£56,713	
Dr	£57,473	
Cr	£57,473	

(c) **The following closing credit balances were in the Subsidiary (purchases) ledger on 30 June.**

Reconcile the balances shown above with the Purchases ledger control account balance you have calculated in part (a).

	£
Gardens Unlimited	15,620
P Lower	1,695
L Brown	23,000
White Brothers	16,200
Hoe and Dig	578

	£
Purchase ledger control account balance as at 30 June 2005	
Total of Subsidiary (purchases) ledger accounts as at 30 June 2005	
Difference	

(d) **What may have caused the difference you calculated in part (c)?**

	✓
Goods bought on credit have been omitted from Subsidiary (purchases) ledger	
Discounts received have been omitted from the Subsidiary (purchases) ledger	
Goods returned have been entered twice in the Subsidiary (purchases) ledger	
Discounts received have been entered twice in the Subsidiary (purchases) ledger	

Task 2.18

On 28 June The Garden Warehouse received the following bank statement as at 24 June.

MIDDLE BANK PLC

12 High Street, Droitwich, WR15 7LW

To: The Garden Warehouse   Account No: 39287594   24 June 2005

STATEMENT OF ACCOUNT

Date 2005	Details	Paid out £	Paid in £	Balance £	Tick
1 June	Balance b/f			15,619 C	
6 June	Cheque 008301	2,650		12,969 C	
8 June	Cheque 008302	1,986		10,983 C	
10 June	Bank Giro Credit A Parker		550	11,533 C	
10 June	Bank Giro Credit L Westwood		6,140	17,673 C	
13 June	Cheque 008303	8,432		9,241 C	
15 June	Direct Debit Droitwich CC	100		9,141 C	
20 June	Direct Debit Cranston Insurance	250		8,891 C	
22 June	Overdraft facility fee	50		8,841 C	
22 June	Bank charges	16		8,825 C	
22 June	Bank interest		26	8,851 C	

D = Debit   C = Credit

The Cash book as at 28 June 2005 is shown below.

Cash book

Date 2005	Details	Tick	Bank £	Date 2005	Cheque Number	Details	Tick	Bank £
1 June	Balance b/f		15,619	1 June	008301	Portman Brothers		2,650
10 June	A Parker		550	1 June	008302	Tether & Tie		1,986
10 June	L Westwood		6,140	6 June	008303	D Price		8,432
15 June	CCC Ltd		1,260	6 June	008304	Mundon Ltd		1,407
22 June	B Williams		142	22 June	008305	Hackett Ltd		350
				28 June		Balance c/d		
29 June	Balance b/d							

(a)   **Check the items on the bank statement against the items in the cash book, ticking each item that matches.**

(b)   **Enter any items in the cash book as needed.**

(c)   **Total the cash book and clearly show the balance carried down at 28 June (closing balance) and brought down at 29 June (opening balance).**

Note: **you do not need to adjust the accounts in Section 1.**

(d)   Now complete the bank reconciliation statement as at 28 June. Do not make any entries in the shaded boxes.

Bank reconciliation statement as at 28 June 2005		
Balance as per bank statement		£
Add:		
	Name:	£
	Name:	£
Total to add		£
Less:		
	Name:	£
	Name:	£
Total to subtract		£
Balance as per cash book		£

Task 2.19

This is an order from a customer of The Garden Warehouse. The goods were delivered on 1 July and all documentation is in order. The discount policy is to offer a 2% settlement discount on all orders over £1,000 excluding VAT.

TGL Limited
The Avenue, Broadway, West Midlands, B84 3LD
Order No: 290

To: The Garden Warehouse
Date: 17 June 2005

Please supply 500 heavy duty gardening forks code F60 at £12 each plus VAT as per your quotation.

Prepare the sales invoice below.

The Garden Warehouse
2a Lower Parade
Droitwich
Worcestershire, WR16 8IS
VAT Registration No. 387 2987 00

Invoice No: 853

Your Order No:

Date:

Quantity	Description	Product code	Net £	VAT £	Total £

2% settlement discount for payment within 7 days

Task 2.20

On 1 July Swindon Spades, a customer of The Garden Warehouse, has an amount outstanding in the subsidiary ledger of £3,525. This relates to invoice number 110 dated 16 January 2005.

Draft a letter from Marian Walker requesting payment of the overdue account by return.

The Garden Warehouse
2a Lower Parade
Droitwich
Worcestershire, WR16 8IS

Swindon Spades
18 High Street
Swindon
FR3 1JH

Practice Examination 2
Premier Space

PRACTICE EXAMINATION 2
PREMIER SPACE

This exam paper is in TWO sections.

You should therefore attempt and aim to complete EVERY task in EACH section.

Section 1   Double entry bookkeeping and trial balance

Complete all 10 tasks

Section 2   Accounting processes

Complete all 20 tasks and questions

You should spend about 75 minutes on Section 1 and about 105 minutes on Section 2.

Both sections are based on the business described below.

INTRODUCTION

- John McVee is the owner of an advertising business, which trades as Premier Space.

- You are employed by the business as a bookkeeper.

- The business uses a manual accounting system.

- Double entry takes place in the Main (General) ledger. Individual accounts of debtors and creditors are kept in subsidiary ledgers as memorandum accounts.

- Bank payments and receipts are recorded in the cash book, which is part of the double entry system.

- Assume today's date is 30 November 2005 unless you are told otherwise.

Section 1 – Double entry bookkeeping and trial balance

You should spend about 75 minutes on this section.

Note: **you should show your answer by inserting a tick, text or figures, as appropriate.**

Task 1.1

On 1 November there were opening balances on all the accounts in the Subsidiary (purchases) ledger, which represented amounts owing by Premier Space.

Would these balances be debit or credit balances?

	✓
Debit	
Credit	

Task 1.2

On 30 November the following opening balances were in the Main ledger.

Would the opening balances in the Main ledger be shown as a debit or credit entry?

Account name	Amount	Debit	Credit
	£	✓	✓
Purchases	286,000		
Purchases returns	2,915		
Purchases ledger control	39,874		
Motor vehicles	4,610		
Stationery	180		
Rent and rates	1,758		
Motor tax	180		

Task 1.3

The following transactions all took place on 30 November 2005 and have been entered into the Purchases day book as shown below. No entries have yet been made into the ledger system.

Purchases day book

Date 2005	Details	Invoice Number	Total £	VAT at 17.5% £	Net £
30 Nov	Brown Ltd	P129	7,050	1,050	6,000
30 Nov	Clarke and Crown	1983	3,525	525	3,000
30 Nov	PPV Ltd	Z120	10,575	1,575	9,000
30 Nov	Lees Ltd	398	5,875	875	5,000
	Totals		27,025	4,025	23,000

(a) **What will be the entries in the Subsidiary (purchases) ledger?**

Account name	Amount £	Debit ✓	Credit ✓

(b) **What will be the entries in the Main ledger?**

Account name	Amount £	Debit ✓	Credit ✓

Task 1.4

The following transactions all took place on 30 November 2005 and have been entered into the Purchases returns day book as shown below. No entries have yet been made into the ledger system.

Purchases returns day book

Date 2005	Details	Credit Note Number	Total £	VAT at 17.5% £	Net £
30 Nov	Brown Ltd	CN19	47	7	40
30 Nov	PPV Ltd	CZ28	188	28	160
	Totals		235	35	200

(a)   What will be the entries in the Subsidiary (purchases) ledger?

Account name	Amount £	Debit ✓	Credit ✓

(b)   What will be the entries in the Main ledger?

Account name	Amount £	Debit ✓	Credit ✓

Task 1.5

The following transactions all took place on 30 November 2005 and have been entered into the Sales day book as shown below. No entries have yet been made into the ledger system.

Sales day book

Date 2005	Details	Invoice Number	Total £	VAT at 17.5% £	Net £
30 Nov	L Grainger	3170	17,625	2,625	15,000
30 Nov	C Hodgetts	3171	2,115	315	1,800
30 Nov	Baynham Ltd	3172	2,350	350	2,000
30 Nov	Castle & Co	3173	4,700	700	4,000
	Totals		26,790	3,990	22,800

(a)   What will be the entries in the Subsidiary (sales) ledger?

Account name	Amount £	Debit ✓	Credit ✓

(b)   What will be the entries in the Main ledger?

Account name	Amount £	Debit ✓	Credit ✓

Task 1.6

The following transactions all took place on 30 November 2005 and have been entered into the cash book as shown below. No entries have yet been made into the ledger system.

Cash book

Date 2005	Details	Bank £	Date 2005	Cheque Details	VAT £	Bank £
30 Nov	Balance b/f	15,021	30 Nov	Motor vehicle		6,000
			30 Nov	Stationery	14	94
			30 Nov	Rent and rates		200
			30 Nov	Motor tax		90
			30 Nov	Clarke and Crown		1,500
				(creditor)		
				Balance c/d		7,137
		15,021				15,021
1 Dec	Balance b/d	7,137				

What will be the entries to record these payments in the Subsidiary (purchases) ledger and Main ledger?

Subsidiary (purchases) ledger

Account name	Amount £	Debit ✓	Credit ✓

Main ledger

Account name	Amount £	Debit ✓	Credit ✓

Task 1.7

The following two accounts are in the main ledger at the close of day on 30 November.

(a)   **Insert the balance carried down together with date and details.**

(b)   **Insert the totals.**

(c)   **Insert the balance brought down together with date and details.**

Advertising

Date 2005	Details	Amount £	Date 2005	Details	Amount £
01 Nov	Balance b/f	600			
26 Nov	Bank	1,200			
	Total			Total	

Fixtures and fittings

Date 2005	Details	Amount £	Date 2005	Details	Amount £
01 Nov	Balance b/f	11,000	29 Nov	Journal correction	500
22 Nov	Bank	1,000			
	Total			Total	

Task 1.8

Record the journal entries needed in the Main ledger to deal with the following items.

Note: You do not need to give narratives. You may not need to use all the lines.

(a)   An amount of £85 has been debited to the insurance account instead of the telephone expenses account.

Account name	Amount £	Debit ✓	Credit ✓

(b)   Premier Space buy from and sell to Protem Ltd. Entries are to be made in the Main ledger to record a contra payment of £200.

Account name	Amount £	Debit ✓	Credit ✓

(c)   A credit customer, J Rowland Ltd, has ceased trading. It owes Premier Space £800 plus VAT. The net amount and VAT must be written off in the Main ledger.

Account name	Amount £	Debit ✓	Credit ✓

Task 1.9

During the month a trial balance was extracted which did not balance and an amount of £60 was credited to the suspense account. The following two errors have now been discovered.

(i)   An amount of £40 has been omitted from the discounts allowed account.

(ii)   A payment of £900 has been recorded as £1,000 in the travel expenses account.

What entries are needed in the Main ledger to correct these errors?

Note: You may not need to use all the lines.

Account name	Amount £	Debit ✓	Credit ✓

Task 1.10

Below is a list of balances to be transferred to the trial balance as at 30 November.

Place the figures in the debit or credit column, as appropriate, and total each column.

Account name	Amount £	Debit £	Credit £
Motor vehicles	10,610		
Fixtures and fittings	11,500		
Stock	20,000		
Cash at bank	7,137		
Petty cash control	120		
Sales ledger control	106,842		
Purchases ledger control	78,150		
VAT owing	14,875		
Capital	25,192		
Sales	400,500		
Sales returns	300		
Purchases	309,000		
Purchases returns	3,115		
Discount allowed	220		
Wages	45,400		
Insurance	900		
Motor tax	270		
Rent and rates	1,958		
Travel expenses	1,928		
Stationery	260		
Printing	750		
Advertising	1,800		
Telephone	312		
Professional fees	1,105		
Bad debts written off	800		
Miscellaneous expenses	620		
Totals			

Section 2 – Accounting processes

You should spend about 105 minutes on this section.

Note 1: You do not need to adjust any accounts in Section 1 as part of any of the following tasks.

Note 2: You should show your answer by inserting a tick, text or figures, as appropriate.

Task 2.1

You have been asked to calculate the amount of VAT owing to HM Revenue & Customs for the last VAT quarter. All sales and purchases are subject to VAT at 17.5%.

(a)   **Complete the VAT calculation summary below.**

VAT calculation summary		
Sales £180,000 **excluding** VAT	VAT on sales	£
Purchases £111,625 **including** VAT	VAT on purchases	£
	VAT payable	£

(b)   **What will be the accounting entries required to record payment of this amount by cheque?**

Account name	Debit ✓	Credit ✓

Task 2.2

John McVee is considering buying some new office equipment and has asked the bank for an overdraft facility.

(a)   **What is an overdraft facility?**

	✓
An interest free loan	
A form of borrowing where the current account can be overdrawn up to an agreed amount	
A credit card facility	

(b) Would the overdraft show in the trial balance of Premier Space as a debit or credit balance?

	✓
A **debit** balance	
A **credit** balance	

Task 2.3

Premier Space operates a petty cash system with a monthly imprest level of £120. In November £98 was spent from petty cash.

(a) What is the amount required to restore the imprest level?

£

(b) Will the restored amount be recorded on the debit or credit side of the petty cash book?

	✓
Debit	
Credit	

Task 2.4

Insert the missing word in each of the following sentences.

(a) Due to insufficient funds, a cheque from a debtor has been ....by the debtor's bank.
(b) A .... card is used to make a payment electronically from a current account.
(c) A cheque is said to be out of date when it is more than .... months old.

Task 2.5

The accounting records of Premier Space consist of three ledgers: the Main ledger, the Subsidiary (purchases) ledger and the Subsidiary (sales) ledger.

In which ledger would you find the following accounts?

Account name	Ledger
(a) L Jones Ltd (a supplier)	
(b) Loan from bank	
(c) Sales returns	
(d) Discounts received	

Task 2.6

Premier Space makes payments by standing order and direct debit.

State which payment method would be the most appropriate for the following.

Type of payment	Standing order ✓	Direct debit ✓
Monthly telephone bill with varying amounts payable each month.		
Repayment of loan at a rate of £100 per month for 12 months.		
Quarterly insurance of between £500 and £600 per quarter.		

Task 2.7

Name THREE checks you would make before authorising a supplier's invoice for payment.

(i)	
(ii)	
(iii)	

Task 2.8

The net wages paid to employees in November were made up of the elements shown below.

Would each element be a debit or credit entry in the Wages and salaries control account in the Main ledger?

Account name	Debit ✓	Credit ✓
Net wages paid to employees		
Trade union fees deducted		
Employees' NIC		
Gross wages		

Task 2.9

Premier Space's transactions in November included the items listed below.

State whether each is a capital transaction or a revenue transaction.

Transaction	Capital ✓	Revenue ✓
Purchase of a new computer		
Repair to damaged office window		
Replacement of worn tyres on delivery van		

Task 2.10

In order for a contract to be legal there has to be an offer and acceptance.

Name ONE other essential element of a contract.

| |
| |

Task 2.11

Name TWO source documents from which a sales invoice might be prepared.

| (i) |
| |
| (ii) |

Task 2.12

Premier Space has been offered a 10% discount off the supply of goods if the order is over £1,000.

What is the name of this type of discount?

	✓
Settlement discount	
Trade discount	
Bulk discount	

Task 2.13

Premier Space uses code numbers within the accounting system, for example customer account codes.

Give THREE other examples of how code numbers may be used within the accounting system.

| (i) |
| |
| (ii) |
| (iii) |

Task 2.14

During November there was a random check of cash in the petty cash box against the balance shown in the petty cash book. There was £67 in cash but the balance in the petty cash book was £72.

Suggest THREE possible reasons for this discrepancy.

(i)	
(ii)	
(iii)	

Task 2.15

Premier Space usually places orders for goods by posting them to its suppliers.

Suggest THREE alternative ways of placing orders for goods.

(i)	
(ii)	
(iii)	

Task 2.16

A cheque has been received at Premier Space with the words **account payee only** in the crossing.

What is the effect of these words?

	✓
The cheque can only be paid into Premier Space's bank account	
The cheque can be paid into any bank account	
The cheque can be cashed at the bank	

Task 2.17

This is a summary of transactions with customers during the month of November.

(a)   **Show whether each entry will be a debit or credit in the Sales ledger control account in the Main ledger.**

Account name	Amount	Debit	Credit
	£	✓	✓
Balance of debtors at 1 November 2005	£98,600		
Goods sold on credit	£41,642		
Money received from credit customers	£33,100		
Discounts allowed	£200		
Goods returned by credit customers	£100		

(b)   **What will be the balance brought down on 1 December on the above account?**

		✓
Dr	£106,842	
Cr	£106,842	
Dr	£107,242	
Cr	£107,242	
Dr	£90,358	
Cr	£90,358	

The following opening balances were in the Subsidiary (sales) ledger on 1 December.

	£	
Black and Company	29,383	Debit
Arrowsmith Ltd	14,005	Debit
Gayfield Solicitors	250	Credit
BLK Ltd	17,050	Debit
Rosso and Company	23,362	Debit
Broadbents Ltd	22,792	Debit

(c)   **Reconcile the balances shown above with the Sales ledger control account balance you have calculated in part (a).**

	£
Sales ledger control account balance as at 1 December 2005	
Total of Subsidiary (sales) ledger accounts as at 1 December 2005	
Difference	

(d)   **What may have caused the difference you calculated in part (b)?**

	✓
Goods returned have been omitted from Subsidiary (sales) ledger	
Discounts allowed have been omitted from the Subsidiary (sales) ledger	
The Subsidiary (sales) ledger amount for Gayfield Solicitors could have been a debit balance	
Discounts allowed have been entered twice in the Subsidiary (sales) ledger	

Task 2.18

On 23 November Premier Space received the following bank statement as at 18 November.

	CENTRAL BANK PLC			
	52 The Parade, Darton, DF10 9SW			
To: Premier Space	**Account No. 38920483**		**18 November 2005**	
	STATEMENT OF ACCOUNT			

Date	Details	Paid out	Paid in	Balance
2005		£	£	£
01 Nov	Balance b/f			20,199C
01 Nov	Cheque 600020	199		20,000C
04 Nov	Cheque 600023	2,800		17,200C
08 Nov	Cheque 600024	155		17,045C
09 Nov	Cheque 600026	250		16,795C
10 Nov	Bank Giro Credit			
	B & B Ltd		4,800	21,595C
16 Nov	Cheque 600028	89		21,506C
16 Nov	Direct Debit			
	MBC	370		21,136C
17 Nov	Direct Debit			
	Bray & Co	5,000		16,136C
18 Nov	Bank charges	25		16,111C
18 Nov	Bank Giro Credit			
	Guest Ltd		1,825	17,936C

D = Debit   C = Credit

The cash book as at 23 November 2005 is shown below.

Cash book

Date 2005	Details	Bank £	Date 2005	Cheque Number	Details	Bank £
01 Nov	Balance b/f	20,000	01 Nov	600023	Baker Ltd	2,800
10 Nov	Smith & Jones	1,100	04 Nov	600024	Brown & Co	155
14 Nov	ALO Associates	1,250	04 Nov	600025	Potters Ltd	75
			04 Nov	600026	Roberts & Co	250
			10 Nov	600027	Baxter Ltd	118
			10 Nov	600028	Cox & Co	89
			16 Nov		MBC	370

(a) Check the items on the bank statement against the items in the cash book.

(b) Enter any items in the cash book as needed.

(c) Total the cash book and clearly show the balance carried down at 23 November (closing balance) **and** brought down at 24 November (opening balance).

Note: You do not need to adjust the accounts in Section 1.

(d) Now complete the bank reconciliation statement on the next page as at 23 November. Do not make any entries in the shaded boxes.

Bank reconciliation statement as at 23 November 2005		
Balance as per bank statement		£
Add:		
	Name:	£
	Name:	£
Total to add		£
Less:		
	Name:	£
	Name:	£
Total to subtract		£
Balance as per cash book		£

Task 2.19

The following is a summary of transactions with Bevan & Co, one of Premier Space's credit customers.

£235 re invoice 3142 of 19 October 2005
£940 re invoice 3143 of 15 November 2005
Cheque for £235 received 17 November 2005

Prepare the statement of account below.

<table>
<tr><td colspan="5" align="center">Premier Space
9 The Parklands
Darton
DF10 8FPW

Telephone No. 01403 198473</td></tr>
<tr><td colspan="5">To: Bevan & Co
    29 High Arden Road
    Manchester
    M10 8WT

Date:</td></tr>
<tr><td>Date
2005</td><td>Details</td><td>Invoice
£</td><td>Payment
£</td><td>Amount outstanding
£</td></tr>
<tr><td></td><td></td><td></td><td></td><td></td></tr>
<tr><td></td><td></td><td></td><td></td><td></td></tr>
<tr><td></td><td></td><td></td><td></td><td></td></tr>
<tr><td></td><td></td><td></td><td></td><td></td></tr>
<tr><td></td><td></td><td></td><td></td><td></td></tr>
</table>

Task 2.20

Premier Space has received the following invoice. It has not been authorised by John McVee, as he negotiated a 10% trade discount with Bradbury Boards, which has been omitted from the invoice.

Bradbury Boards
12 High Street
Bradbury
BN15 8DP

Telephone and fax: 01827 388002

VAT Registration No. 874 3672 00

Premier Space
9 The Parklands
Darton
DF10 8PW

Invoice No P1094

Date and tax point: 28 November 2005

100..Best quality pre-printed boards at £100 each	£10,000
VAT at 17.5%	£1,750
Total	£11,750

Draft a letter from John McVee requesting a credit note by return.

**Premier Space
9 The Parklands
Darton
DF10 8PW**

Telephone No. 01403 198473

Bradbury Boards
12 High Street
Bradbury
BN15 8DP

_____

_____

_____

_____

_____

_____

_____

_____

_____

_____

_____

_____

Practice Examination 3
The Clothes Factory

PRACTICE EXAMINATION 3
THE CLOTHES FACTORY

This exam paper is in TWO sections.

You must show competence in BOTH sections.

You should therefore attempt and aim to complete EVERY task in EACH section.

Section 1   Double entry bookkeeping and trial balance

Complete all 10 tasks

Section 2   Accounting processes

Complete all 20 tasks and questions

You should spend about 75 minutes on Section 1 and about 105 minutes on Section 2.

All essential calculations should be included within your answer, where appropriate.

Both sections are based on the business described below.

INTRODUCTION

- Anita Sunil is the owner of a business which wholesales clothes and trades as The Clothes Factory.

- You are employed by the business as a bookkeeper.

- The business uses a manual accounting system.

- Double entry takes place in the Main (General) Ledger. Individual accounts of debtors and creditors are kept in subsidiary ledgers as memorandum accounts.

- Bank payments and receipts are recorded in the cash-book, which is part of the double entry system.

- Assume today's date is 30 June 2007 unless you are told otherwise.

Section 1 – Double entry bookkeeping and trial balance

You should spend about 75 minutes on this section.

Note: **you should show your answer by inserting a tick, text or figures, as appropriate.**

Task 1.1

On 1 June there were opening balances on all the accounts in the Subsidiary (sales) ledger, which represented amounts owed to The Clothes Factory.

Would these balances be debit or credit balances?

	✓
Debit	
Credit	

Task 1.2

On 30 June the following opening balances were in the Main ledger.

Would the opening balances in the Main ledger be shown as a debit or credit entry?

Account name	Amount £	Debit ✓	Credit ✓
Sales	263,895		
Sales returns	3,855		
Sales ledger control	40,293		
Office equipment	10,220		
Discount received	450		
Wages	29,341		
Rent and rates	4,760		

Task 1.3

The following transactions all took place on 30 June 2007 and have been entered into the Sales day book as shown below. No entries have yet been made into the ledger system.

Sales day book

Date 2007	Details	Invoice Number	Total £	VAT at 17.5% £	Net £
30 June	Aziz and Company	591	2,350	350	2,000
30 June	AJS Ltd	592	4,700	700	4,000
30 June	Smythe and Sims	593	5,875	875	5,000
30 June	Choudhury Ltd	594	3,525	525	3,000
	Totals		16,450	2,450	14,000

(a) What will be the entries in the Subsidiary (sales) ledger?

Account name	Amount £	Debit ✓	Credit ✓

(b) What will be the entries in the Main ledger?

Account name	Amount £	Debit ✓	Credit ✓

Task 1.4

On 30 June 2007 there were two sales returns transactions which have not yet been entered into the day book and the ledger system:

- from Hart Ltd for £40 + VAT (credit note CN48 issued)
- from Aziz and Company for £120 + VAT (credit note CN49 issued)

(a) **Insert the date, details, credit note number, total, VAT and net into the following sales returns day book.**

(b) **Insert the totals.**

Sales returns day book

Date 2007	Details	Credit Note Number	Total £	VAT at 17.5% £	Net £
	Totals				

(c) **What will be the entries in the Subsidiary (sales) ledger?**

Account name	Amount £	Debit ✓	Credit ✓

(d) **What will be the entries in the Main ledger?**

Account name	Amount £	Debit ✓	Credit ✓

Task 1.5

The following transactions all took place on 30 June 2007 and have been entered into the Purchases day book as shown below. No entries have yet been made into the ledger system.

Purchases day book

Date 2007	Details	Invoice Number	Total £	VAT at 17.5% £	Net £
30 June	Grainger and Company	3954	1,880	280	1,600
30 June	Chow and Tang	67891	2,350	350	2,000
30 June	P Patel Ltd	6/1468	9,870	1,470	8,400
30 June	TT Ltd	TT379	5,640	840	4,800
	Totals		19,740	2,940	16,800

(a)   What will be the entries in the Subsidiary (purchases) ledger?

Account name	Amount £	Debit ✓	Credit ✓

(b)   What will be the entries in the Main ledger?

Account name	Amount £	Debit ✓	Credit ✓

Task 1.6

The following transactions all took place on 30 June 2007 and have been entered into the cash book as shown below. No entries have yet been made into the ledger system.

Cash book

Date 2007	Details	Bank £	Date 2007	Cheque Details	VAT £	Bank £
30 June	Balance b/f	7,240	30 June	Office equipment	140	940
30 June	Aziz and Company	1,175	30 June	Rent and rates		1,320
	(debtor)		30 June	Telephone expenses	28	188
			30 June	Petty cash control		110
			30 June	Grainger and Company		893
				(creditor)		
				Balance c/d		4,964
		8,415			168	8,415
1 July	Balance b/d	4,964				

What will be the entries to record these payments in the Subsidiary (sales) ledger, the Subsidiary (purchases) ledger, and the Main ledger?

Subsidiary (sales) ledger

Account name	Amount £	Debit ✓	Credit ✓

Subsidiary (purchases) ledger

Account name	Amount £	Debit ✓	Credit ✓

Main ledger

Account name	Amount £	Debit ✓	Credit ✓

Task 1.7

The following two accounts are in the main ledger at the close of day on 30 June 2007.

(a) Insert the balance carried down together with date and details.

(b) Insert the totals.

(c) Insert the balance brought down together with date and details.

Stationery

Date 2007	Details	Amount £	Date 2007	Details	Amount £
1 June	Balance b/f	1,100			
26 June	Bank	500			
	Total			Total	

Petty cash control

Date 2007	Details	Amount £	Date 2007	Details	Amount £
1 June	Balance b/f	200	30 June	Petty cash book	110
30 June	Bank	110			
	Total			Total	

Task 1.8

Record the journal entries needed in the Main ledger to deal with the following items.

Note: You do not need to give narratives. You may not need to use all the lines.

(a)   An amount of £120 has been debited to the miscellaneous expenses account instead of the telephone expenses account.

Account name	Amount £	Debit ✓	Credit ✓

(b)   Sales returns of £100 have been entered as £1,000 in the Main ledger accounts (ignore VAT).

Account name	Amount £	Debit ✓	Credit ✓

(c)   A credit customer, JA Ltd, has ceased trading. It owes The Clothes Factory £400 plus VAT. The net amount and VAT must be written off in the Main ledger.

Account name	Amount £	Debit ✓	Credit ✓

Task 1.9

During the month a trial balance was extracted which did not balance and an amount of £147 was debited to the suspense account. The following two errors have now been discovered.

(i)   An amount of £120 has been omitted from the wages account

(ii)   A payment of £85 has been recorded as £58 in the miscellaneous expenses account.

What entries are needed in the Main ledger to correct these errors?

Note: You may not need to use all the lines.

Account name	Amount £	Debit ✓	Credit ✓

Task 1.10

Below is a list of balances to be transferred to the trial balance as at 30 June.

Place the figures in the debit or credit column, as appropriate, and total each column.

Account name	Amount £	Debit £	Credit £
Office equipment	11,020		
Vehicles	20,500		
Stock	25,000		
Cash at bank	4,964		
Petty cash control	200		
Sales ledger control	55,810		
Purchases ledger control	30,350		
VAT owing	8,400		
Loan from bank	10,000		
Capital	31,938		
Sales	277,895		
Sales returns	3,115		
Purchases	193,900		
Purchases returns	2,545		
Discount received	450		
Discount allowed	290		
Wages	32,411		
Insurance	1,120		
Vehicle expenses	565		
Rent and rates	6,080		
Stationery	1,600		
Heat and light	1,540		
Telephone expenses	735		
Accountancy fees	1,425		
Bad debts written off	400		
Miscellaneous expenses	903		
Totals			

Section 2 – Accounting processes

You should spend about 105 minutes on this section.

Note 1: **You do not need to adjust any accounts in Section 1 as part of any of the following tasks.**

Note 2: **You should show your answer by inserting a tick, text or figures, as appropriate.**

Task 2.1

A trainee asks for your help in the preparation of a sales invoice. She has worked out that the goods total of the invoice, after the deduction of trade discount, is £1,200.00 but, having reached this point, she cannot go any further with the calculation. She has been told that the customer is normally allowed a settlement discount of 2.5% for payment within seven days, otherwise net 30 days.

(a)   What is a settlement discount?   ✓

A discount on the total amount due which applies if the invoice is settled on its due date	
A discount allowed if the invoice is paid within a set number of days earlier than its due date	
A discount allowed on the the total amount due if the goods are being ordered in bulk	

(b)   The VAT amount on the trainee's invoice will be: ✓

£30.00	
£5.25	
£210.00	
£204.75	

Task 2.2

You have been asked to calculate the amount of VAT owing to H M Revenue & Customs for the last VAT quarter. All sales and purchases are subject to VAT at 17.5%.

(a)   Complete the VAT calculation summary below.

VAT calculation summary		
Sales £129,250 **including** VAT	VAT on sales	£
Purchases £62,000 **excluding** VAT	VAT on purchases	£
	VAT payable	£

(b) **What will be the accounting entries required to record payment of this amount by cheque?**

Account name	Debit ✓	Credit ✓

Task 2.3

The Clothes Factory has received the cheque shown below from Gemini Ltd, one of its customers.

Southern Bank PLC
Mereford Branch
16 Broad Street, Mereford MR1 7TR

date 1 June 2007   97-76-54

Pay   The Clothes Factory   only

Four hundred pounds only   £ 450.00

Account payee only

GEMINI LIMITED

123456   977654   68384939

(a) **Give two reasons why this cheque would not be paid by Southern Bank.**

(i)
(ii)

(b) **The 'account payee only' crossing on this cheque means that**   ✓

the cheque can only be paid in if there is money in Gemini Ltd's bank account	
the cheque can only be paid into the account of The Clothes Factory	
the cheque can only be paid into the account of Gemini Ltd	

(c) **If the date were missing from this cheque, it could be filled in by The Clothes Factory**

	✓		✓
TRUE		FALSE	

Task 2.4

What document would The Clothes Factory send to its customer in each of the following circumstances?

		✓
To adjust the customer's account for goods returned	remittance advice	
	credit note	
	invoice	

		✓
To accompany and list goods ordered	statement	
	remittance advice	
	delivery note	

		✓
To advise receipt of an order placed by a customer	receipt	
	order acknowledgement	
	delivery note	

Task 2.5

The Clothes Factory has just opened a credit account for a new customer, Kernow Klothes, which brings the total number of credit customers to 60.

(a)   Suggest an appropriate four-character alphanumeric ledger code for this account.

(b)   In which ledger would you expect to see this account?

	✓
Main ledger	
Subsidiary (sales) ledger	
Subsidiary (purchases) ledger	

Task 2.6

The following errors have been made in the accounting records of The Clothes Factory.

Show whether the errors cause an imbalance in the trial balance by selecting the correct answer.

(a) **An entry has been made to the sales and VAT accounts but omitted from the sales ledger control account.**

	✓
The trial balance will balance	
The trial balance will not balance	

(b) **A purchase invoice has not been entered in the accounting records.**

	✓
The trial balance will balance	
The trial balance will not balance	

(c) **VAT on a sales invoice has been calculated incorrectly.**

	✓
The trial balance will balance	
The trial balance will not balance	

(d) **A sales invoice has been entered in the account of Aziz Ltd instead of M Aziz.**

	✓
The trial balance will balance	
The trial balance will not balance	

Task 2.7

A legal contract must always be in writing to be valid.

	✓
TRUE	
FALSE	

Task 2.8

Which two items from the following do you expect to see in a wages and salaries control account?

✓

VAT payment due to HM Revenue & Customs	
Net wages due to employees	
Payments made by the employer to a national charity	
PAYE amounts deducted from employees' wages	

Task 2.9

A trainee in the Accounts Department at The Clothes Factory brings to your attention a purchase invoice which has an arithmetical error on it. The invoice total should be £450.50 and not £405.50. The trainee makes a number of suggestions, listed below.

State which one course of action you should follow in dealing with this discrepancy.

✓

Do nothing because you will have to pay less and therefore save the company money	
Change the figures on the invoice and pay the correct amount	
Issue a credit note for the difference	
Return the invoice to the supplier, requesting a replacement showing the correct amount	

Task 2.10

Organisations such as The Clothes Factory are making increasing use of the BACS system for making payments.

Which two types of payment from the following would you recommend for processing using BACS?

✓

Payments of wages to permanent employees	
Petty cash imprest 'top-up' payments	
Payments to foreign students who are given short-term casual work by the company	
Payments of amounts owing on Purchase Ledger accounts	

Task 2.11

The Sale of Goods Act gives protection to purchasers of goods in the UK. The law states that the consumer is entitled to certain legal rights when purchasing goods.

Which two conditions in the following list are set out in the Sale of Goods Act?

	✓
Goods must represent 'good value for money'	
Goods must be of 'satisfactory quality'	
Goods must be available to consumers 'on Sundays and official UK public holidays'	
Goods must be 'as described'	

Task 2.12

The Clothes Factory, which has invested heavily in up-to-date computer systems, is considering setting up a separate mail order company, 'Clothes4U', to market and sell its goods to a wide range of private customers.

State three payment methods private customers are likely to use when placing orders with Clothes4U.

(i)
(ii)
(iii)

Task 2.13

The Clothes Factory buys goods from and sells goods to TT Ltd. It has been agreed to set off a debt owing between them by a contra entry.

What accounts in the main ledger of The Clothes Factory would be adjusted to record this set off?

Account name	Debit ✓	Credit ✓

Task 2.14

Transactions for The Clothes Factory in June included the items listed below.

Show whether each is a capital transaction or a revenue transaction.

Transaction	Capital ✓	Revenue ✓
Wages and salaries		
Purchase of property		
Legal fees relating to the purchase of property		
Redecoration of the office		

Task 2.15

The Clothes Factory operates a petty cash imprest system.

(a)   Which ONE of the following statements best describes an imprest system?

	✓
The petty cashier draws money from the main cashier as and when required.	
The main cashier has to authorise each petty cash payment.	
A copy has to be kept of each petty cash voucher.	
The petty cashier starts each week or month with a fixed amount of money.	

(b)   Name another system for operating petty cash.

Task 2.16

Anita Sunil has agreed to buy a secondhand car for £8,000 for business use. The seller does not want to accept a business cheque, in case it is dishonoured, and does not want cash.

(a)   What service offered by banks would you recommend to The Clothes Factory?

| |
| |

(b)   What will be the accounting entries required in the Main ledger to record the purchase?

Account name	Debit ✓	Credit ✓

Task 2.17

This is a summary of transactions with suppliers during the month of June.

(a)   Show whether each entry will be a debit or credit in the Purchases ledger control account in the Main ledger.

Account name	Amount £	Debit ✓	Credit ✓
Balance of creditors at 1 June 2007	40,300		
Goods purchased on credit	21,587		
Money paid to credit suppliers	30,362		
Discounts received	150		
Goods returned to credit suppliers	1,025		

(b) What will be the balance brought down on 1 July on the above account?

		✓
Dr	£32,700	
Cr	£32,700	
Dr	£30,350	
Cr	£30,350	
Dr	£50,250	
Cr	£50,250	

The following opening balances were in the Subsidiary (purchases) ledger on 1 July.

	£	
Grainger and Company	3,105	Credit
TT Ltd	8,226	Credit
Chow and Tang	4,195	Credit
P Patel Ltd	12,246	Credit
BB Traders	500	Debit
L Vakas	2,078	Credit

(c) Reconcile the balances shown above with the Purchases ledger control account balance you have calculated in part (b).

	£
Purchases ledger control account balance as at 1 July 2007	
Total of Subsidiary (purchases) ledger accounts as at 1 July 2007	
Difference	

(d) What may have caused the difference you calculated in part (c)?

	✓
Goods returned have been omitted from Subsidiary (purchases) ledger	
Discounts received have been omitted from the Subsidiary (purchases) ledger	
The Subsidiary (purchases) ledger amount for BB Traders could have been a credit balance	
Discounts received have been entered twice in the Subsidiary (purchases) ledger	

Task 2.18

On 22 June The Clothes Factory received the following bank statement as at 18 June.

WEST BANK PLC

33 High Street, Burngrove, BU1 4UF

To: The Clothes Factory	Account No: 04516835	18 June 2007

STATEMENT OF ACCOUNT

Date	Details	Paid out	Paid in	Balance
2007		£	£	£
01 June	Balance b/f			7,000 C
05 June	Cheque 101605	300		6,700 C
05 June	Cheque 101610	5,500		1,200 C
05 June	Cheque 101611	1,500		300 D
10 June	BACS Credit			
	AJS Ltd		9,100	8,800 C
11 June	Cheque 101613	1,100		7,700 C
14 June	Direct Debit			
	TT Ltd	1,300		6,400 C
15 June	Direct Debit			
	Burngrove District Council	300		6,100 C
18 June	Bank charges	52		6,048 C

D = Debit   C = Credit

The cash book as at 22 June 2007 is shown below.

Cash book

Date 2007	Details	Bank £	Date 2007	Cheque Number	Details	Bank £
01 June	Balance b/f	6,700	01 June	101610	P Patel Ltd	5,500
21 June	Choudhury Ltd	2,100	01 June	101611	Chow and Tang	1,500
26 June	Okara and Associates	650	06 June	101612	Grainger and Company	600
			07 June	101613	Burngrove Motors	1,100
			17 June	101614	L Vakas	245

(a) Check the items on the bank statement against the items in the cash book.

(b) Enter any items in the cash book as needed.

(c) Total the cash book and clearly show the balance carried down at 22 June (closing balance) **and** brought down at 23 June (opening balance).

Note: You do not need to adjust the accounts in Section 1.

(d) Now complete the bank reconciliation statement as at 22 June. Do not make any entries in the shaded boxes.

Bank reconciliation statement as at 22 June 2007	
Balance as per bank statement	£
Add:	
Name:	£
Name:	£
Total to add	£
Less:	
Name:	£
Name:	£
Total to subtract	£
Balance as per cash book	£

Task 2.19

The Clothes Factory has received the purchase order shown below from N Singh Ltd. All routine checks have been carried out.

N Singh Ltd is normally offered a 5% settlement discount on orders over £2,000 (excluding VAT) for payment within seven days.

You are to prepare the invoice, dated 1 July 2007, which is shown on the next page. Complete the details required on the shaded areas. All the other details have been provided.

The VAT rate is 17.5%. Remember to round down the VAT amount to the nearest penny.

N Singh Limited	**PURCHASE ORDER**

17 Masefield Street
Broadfield
BR2 6TG
Tel 01901 3245151 Fax 01901 3245155
VAT REG GB 0831 1228 22

The Clothes Factory,	purchase order no	62721
Unit 46 Marcello Estate,	date	25 06 07
Burngrove,		
BU2 4JH		

product code	quantity	description
T234R	500	T shirts (red) @ £5.00 each

AUTHORISED signature............*N Singh*..date...*25/06/07*......

INVOICE

THE CLOTHES FACTORY

Unit 46 Marcello Estate, Burngrove, BU2 4JH
Tel 01646 765314 Fax 01646 765951 Email sales@clothesfactory.co.uk
VAT Reg GB 0841 2272 43

invoice to

invoice no	**595**
account	**NS525**
your reference	**62721**
date/tax point	**01 07 07**

product code	description	quantity	price	unit	net	VAT	Total

terms
5% settlement discount for payment
within 7 days.

Task 2.20

On 1 July The Clothes Factory receives from Fancy Importers Limited an invoice for a delivery of sweat shirts. When the invoice is checked you find that there is a discrepancy on the invoice. You query the invoice with Anita Sunil who returns it to you with the following note:

"Right goods sent and invoiced, but no 20% trade discount deducted as agreed. Please send an email to salesledger@fancyimporters.co.uk asking for a credit note. Goods total on invoice before VAT was £1,200. Please calculate amount of credit note."

The VAT rate is 17.5%. The invoice number is 27834 and the date of the invoice 25 June 2007.

You are to carry out the necessary calculations and draft the text of an appropriate email in the box below. Your normal contact in the sales ledger section at Fancy Importers is Jocelyn Smith, whom you know as Josie.

email to: salesledger@fancyimporters.co.uk

subject: invoice 27834, dated 25 June 2007

Appendix

Photocopiable layouts

This appendix of photocopiable material comprises the following blank layouts:

- double-entry ledger accounts
- sales day book
- purchases day book
- petty cash book

You are free to photocopy these pages for classroom use, but they remain the copyright of the publisher and authors.

These layouts and a variety of financial documents are available for free download from our website: www.osbornebooks.co.uk

DOUBLE-ENTRY ACCOUNTS

Dr   Cr

Date	Details	Amount	Date	Details	Amount
		£			£

Dr   Cr

Date	Details	Amount	Date	Details	Amount
		£			£

Dr   Cr

Date	Details	Amount	Date	Details	Amount
		£			£

Sales Day Book						SDB
Date	Customer	Invoice No	Folio	Total	VAT	Net
				£	£	£

Purchases Day Book						PDB
Date	Supplier	Invoice No	Folio	Total	VAT	Net
				£	£	£

PETTY CASH BOOK **PCB**

Receipts £	Date	Details	Voucher No	Total Payment £	VAT £	Analysis columns £	£	£	£